SELLING YOUR EXPERTISE

The Mindset, Strategies, and Tactics of Successful Rainmakers

Robert Chen

WILEY

Published by John Wiley & Sons, Inc., Hoboken, New Jersey.
Published simultaneously in Canada.

For general information on our other products and services or for technical support, please contact our Customer Care Department within the United States at (800) 762-2974, outside the United States at (317) 572-3993 or fax (317) 572-4002.

Wiley publishes in a variety of print and electronic formats and by print-on-demand. Some material included with standard print versions of this book may not be included in e-books or in print-on-demand. If this book refers to media such as a CD or DVD that is not included in the version you purchased, you may download this material at http://booksupport.wiley.com. For more information about Wiley products, visit www.wiley.com.

Library of Congress Cataloging-in-Publication Data:

Name: Chen, Robert (Executive Coach), author.

Title: Selling your expertise : the mindset, strategies, and tactics of successful rainmakers / Robert Chen.

Description: Hoboken, New Jersey : Wiley, [2022] | Includes index.

Identifiers: LCCN 2021054272 (print) | LCCN 2021054273 (ebook) | ISBN 9781119755142 (cloth) | ISBN 9781119755272 (adobe pdf) | ISBN 9781119755128 (epub)

Subjects: LCSH: Selling. | Service industries.

Classification: LCC HF5438.25 .C4795 2022 (print) | LCC HF5438.25 (ebook) | DDC 658.85—dc23/eng/20211202

LC record available at https://lccn.loc.gov/2021054272
LC ebook record available at https://lccn.loc.gov/2021054273

Cover image: © Getty Images | Filo
Cover design: Paul McCarthy

SKY10031816_020322

Praise for *Selling Your Expertise*

"The growth of any organization is driven by its sales team and is vital to future success. Selling Your Expertise *shows how a positive approach combined with best practices can increase productivity, output, and ultimately, success. An essential how-to book for professionals in any industry who want to grow their business and build their future."*

—Ken Daly,
President, St. Thomas Aquinas College

"If you are like most highly-educated professionals, selling seems like a foreboding exercise that you must force yourself to do at the inflection point in your career when you suddenly face being evaluated not on your expertise but instead on your ability to generate business. Selling Your Expertise *is a must read for any professional striving to become a rainmaker, anyone who has realized through painful experience that there must be more to selling than schmoozing."*

—John Chou,
former Executive Vice President and
Chief Legal Officer, AmerisourceBergen

"Chen gets it right; rainmaking is essential in virtually all business enterprises. And that skill can be taught and learned."

—Stanley Goldstein,
Chair Emeritus, New York Alternative
Investment Roundtable, Chairman, Sustainability
Investment Leadership Council

"Chen empowers us as professionals to not just deliver our work but to create value by selling. Whether you are a first-timer or a seasoned business developer, new or resistant to selling, Selling Your Expertise *will open your mind and heart to greater career opportunities and rewards. Thank you, Robert!"*

—Jay Persaud,
Vice Chair, Big Four Professional Services Organization

"Building and maintaining lasting client relationships is key for the long-term success of any business. Selling Your Expertise *outlines a clear roadmap with proven strategies to leverage your professional experience and knowledge to serve your clients, build enduring relationships, and scale the business."*

—Srinivas Rapthadu,
Business Transformation Officer,
Global Strategy Consulting Ecosystems, SAP

"Remarkable insights and an in-depth resource for anyone who views a sales role with skepticism or trepidation. I view Selling Your Expertise *as essential reading for anyone in professional services who is serving in a technical role. Here is a practical and realistic guide for building a career roadmap for success."*

—Hiroshi Baensch,
Senior Partner, Mercer

"You can offer the best data, models, and analytical skills in the world, but more important than any of that is the ability to sell your expertise. Robert Chen provides some unique and invaluable lessons, which I find immediately useful for my own teaching and consulting work."

—Professor Peter Fader,
Frances and Pei-Yuan Chia, Professor of Marketing,
The Wharton School of The University of Pennsylvania

"Robert Chen clearly understands the subtleties and nuances of interpersonal dynamics. In Selling Your Expertise, *his advice on how to develop business authentically in your own voice is not to be missed."*

—Michelle Nasir,
Chief Talent Officer, Arsenal Capital Partners

"If there is one book to read on developing selling acumen for someone who is not a 'born salesperson,' Selling Your Expertise *is it. It offers relational guiding principles and step-by-step approaches that help any expert within their business understand how to build a thriving book of business. You'll not only gain practical insights, but the confidence to be a rainmaker!"*

—Paul Wypasek,
Chief Learning Officer, Turner Construction

SELLING YOUR EXPERTISE

To Amy, for always saying, "sure" to my countless pursuits

*To Jake and Jonah, for your unexpected
comments that always make me smile*

Contents

Foreword

In 2017, I was introduced to Robert at a networking event. I do not recall exactly what we discussed, but I do remember that he made a lasting impression—he was prepared, present, and engaged. As often happens at these professional gatherings, we exchanged contact information with the usual pleasantries on following up. The difference here is that Robert *did* reach out to me. Since then, I have been fortunate in partnering with him on presentations in regard to career progression; connecting at alumni gatherings; and watching his leadership in action at Pan-Asian executive events.

Robert is one of the best when it comes to remaining authentic while reading a room, genuinely connecting with others in the moment and building relationships in real-time. He embodies the often-overused term "trusted advisor"—someone you turn to when you have a problem because he provides you with the necessary guidance or knows who can. After learning about his intention to share his knowledge and experience, I am honored that he asked me to write this foreword.

I have sat in multiple seats in the finance world: as a Managing Director in investment banking, a Chief Financial Officer at a public company, and now the Chief Revenue Officer for a leading FinTech firm. My career path is not what I envisioned when I graduated college and joined Salomon Brothers as a programmer, supporting the mortgage bond trading desk. While I enjoyed the technical challenges, I realized career advancement required that I be closer to the revenue generating side of the business. However, for me to feel confident, I wanted to be the subject matter expert. I believed this would give me the "power," the "right," and a clear role to play, even if that meant I was not a lead.

I discovered that while there are advantages in being a technical expert, the client relationship is not only the most gratifying personally but also the most valued professionally. The issue for me, however, was that I did not consider myself a salesperson. I did not believe I had the extroverted personality, the pushiness needed to get quick commitments, or quite frankly, the willingness to take risk and rejection. But what I did have was the work ethic, the capability to read a room, and importantly, a very competitive spirit. These traits provided me the ability to generate a growing book of business, to earn respect from clients, and to successfully progress in my career. Along the way, I learned, observed, and adopted winning practices from my many experienced colleagues.

Looking back, I believe I would have benefitted from being more intentional in my strategies and prepared to execute on them. What Robert's book provides so pointedly is advice on developing such intention and preparation in writing that is both strategic and tactical. He shares how a person can leverage their technical expertise and position themselves to be accountable in generating revenue growth. His sound advice deeply resonates with me. It's a holistic approach: First, there is the importance of *mindset*, which sets the tone. This mindset provides the understanding that anyone can be a rainmaker by accentuating their strengths and developing the mental fortitude to push through often self-imposed obstacles. Second, there is a need for *strategy* in business development, which requires a longer-term view but also a purposeful one that considers client needs *as well as* one's personal goals. And lastly, there is the criticality of *tactics*, which ultimately can seem like a daily grind of tedium and common sense but is the true X-factor—because in the end, it's all about the execution.

Success is a continuous learning process. Our experiences shape us, and we each benefit from taking stock on both our successes and failures. Robert's book contains the right balance of candor, theory, and practicality to help you take stock of your career progression, transition or accelerate into a rainmaker, and succeed in sales. While his intention may be to target those who are mid-level in their careers, I found myself actively agreeing with key points and pausing to consider whether I was in need of such reassessment as well. As Robert notes in Chapter 13, "If you stop taking risks, you stop learning."

Business development can be incredibly rewarding and challenging. If you have a desire to meet your fullest professional potential, *Selling Your Expertise* will guide you along the way. Its thought-provoking and action-oriented advice can help you fulfill your career objectives and lead you to a thriving book of business.

Helen Shan
EVP and Chief Revenue Officer
FactSet Research Systems Ltd.

Introduction

I never thought I would be in sales.

Growing up, I didn't know anyone who aspired to become a "salesperson." Culturally, as a first-generation Chinese-American, I was under the impression that sales was the white-collar job you took only if you couldn't find any other. This belief was reinforced when I took my first official sales gig during a summer break in college. Prior to that summer, my only work experience had been in a material science lab researching electro-conducting polymers. It seemed like a good idea to take on a part-time job doing something different to see what other options were out there, and to supplement my research stipend. Coincidently, right before break, I received an unsolicited letter from Vector Marketing inviting me to interview for their summer work program. The letter mentioned the company had been established in 1981, and they were expanding. Then I read the magic words: base salary $17.00 per hour. At the time, minimum wage was just $5.15.

I'd never heard of Vector Marketing, and it wasn't clear what the job was all about, but I decided to show up for my interview anyway. After a long wait in the lobby with several other candidates, and a rather unexceptional interview, I was offered the position on the spot. I envisioned on-the-job learning, market research, and working on a team, so I was surprised when I finally learned what the job actually entailed—selling Cutco kitchen knives.

Feeling somewhat tricked, but also intrigued by the high compensation, I decided to give it a go. I accepted the offer, received my sample knife set, and attended training. I learned the standard sales pitch, which included showcasing the most popular knives and cutting a penny into a swan using Cutco's powerful scissors. After training, I was sent on a sales ride-along with a more seasoned Cutco rep. He made the role look easy. He sold a knife set at two of the three appointments we went to. Then I was tasked to go off on my own.

I failed miserably. I gave the presentation to my immediate family, relatives, friends' parents, and anyone else who would listen to me, cutting penny after penny into beautiful swans, but I could not make a sale. (I might have been better off trying to sell those swans for a nickel). Finally, my uncle took pity on me and bought a set of knives, but he sheepishly called me to return them later that day once my aunt heard about it.

Throughout this process, I felt uncomfortable pushing for the sale or even asking for referrals. I blamed my poor performance on the high cost of those knives, and I griped that Chinese immigrant families do not use seven different kitchen knives—we only use cleavers. All I salvaged from the job was my sample knife set, which still sits on my parents' kitchen counter. However, I keep the swan-cutting scissors on the desk in my office as a reminder that quality products do not sell themselves. (They also happen to come in handy for opening those annoying hard plastic packages.)

This entire experience validated what I already knew: Sales was not for me. Later in my career, after I'd realized this was entirely untrue, I began to recognize this same distaste for sales from many of my professional services clients. I've heard a junior principal at a top management consulting firm say, "I'm not a sales guy. I know my strengths, and I'm focusing on what I do best." Ultimately, he moved into a non–client facing role, which felt more comfortable to him, but ended up limiting his advancement within his firm. An investment banker at a top-tier firm once told me he was leaving to go where his skills were appreciated, but only after he wasn't nominated for Managing Director because of his limited success in sourcing business. And then there was the senior manager at a Big Four accounting firm who said, "They deferred me for partnership this year because my business case wasn't strong enough." Without bringing in new clients, partnership was out of reach for her.

Delivering and Selling

If these sentiments sound familiar to you, you're not alone. Like countless others, you may have found yourself at a crossroads in your career. You know you are good at what you do, and you take pride in your work, but you've realized that your technical expertise alone won't help you get ahead. Like most professionals, there is a good chance you have spent your career focused on developing your expertise and delivering work to your clients. If you are a lawyer, you draft documents or analyze cases, spending most of your time on billable work. As a portfolio manager, you listen to earnings calls and read quarterly filings to find strong investments for your clients. And as a management consultant, you scrutinize your client's processes and present them with more profitable strategies (whether they listen to you and follow through or not is another story).

As you aspire to the top of your firm, it will quickly become clear that *simply delivering the technical work is not enough*. If you look closely at your firm's most successful leaders, they likely spend much of their time building relationships and bringing in business. But they do more than just occasionally or randomly sell their skills and expertise or their company's services—they make it rain.

By definition, rainmakers sell more than the average professional. They are consistently the top revenue generators for their firm, despite the economy, a worldwide pandemic, or fierce competition. Rainmakers are made, not born, and they only get to their level of success by first crossing the chasm from *delivering* their work to *delivering and selling* their work.

The shift from delivering the work to delivering *and* selling the work can often be intimidating, not to mention frustrating. People going through this experience resist this change and often ask, "Why do I need to do that? That's not the job I signed up for," or argue, "A good product or service sells itself." Another line you may have heard: "I didn't become a [insert profession] so that I could knock on doors." These protests mask the real reason for the frustration—doubt and insecurity about one's ability to sell. It also doesn't help that most people are not taught *how* to sell.

If you are an introvert by nature, or if building relationships is just not your forte, you may struggle to imagine yourself ever becoming a rainmaker. The leap from delivering the work to selling the work might even appear overly risky and unachievable. Even for those who have bridged that divide, they may still see business development as a never-ending, unpleasant, yet necessary activity they must engage in as the price for doing what they "really" enjoy, the substantive work.

Many technical experts see selling as a deviation from their "real" work. In reality, it's not a deviation but an *evolution*. The goal here is not to become a professional salesperson but rather a professional who can sell. That means uncovering engagement opportunities and instilling confidence in your prospective clients to win those opportunities. Continued success depends partly on your technical expertise, of course, but ultimately, it boils down to adopting the mindset, mastering the strategies, and employing the tactics that are at the heart of successful rainmaking.

Throughout this book, I walk you through these three components, highlighting practical insights and actionable advice to help you successfully build and sustainably cultivate a strong book of business. Everything you read here is backed by research, empirical evidence, and first-hand interviews and experience.

What It Means to Sell

At Exec|Comm, a global skills-based training consultancy, my colleagues and I are often engaged to work with professionals who have tremendous subject-matter expertise. We help them broaden the contributions they make to their organizations by sharpening their business development and communication skills. During these engagements, we regularly find that many technically gifted professionals have an inaccurate understanding of what it means to sell.

For example, when we ask mid-level investment bankers how we might help them build more business, they regularly say something along the lines of, "I have a meeting coming up with an executive at a Fortune 100 company. They are only meeting with me because they are a friend of my managing director. How can I connect with this person so that it is not just a courtesy call?" Another typical response we hear includes something like, "When I'm meeting with someone I know socially, how do I transition to talking about work? I know they're in a position to hire my firm, but I don't want to jeopardize our friendship." These professionals assume that selling is all about networking effectively, building rapport, and entertaining clients. Although these activities can certainly play a part, there is much more to selling than schmoozing.

Exec|Comm's philosophy is that success comes from focusing less on yourself and more on others. When applied to selling your expertise, this means thinking of selling not as pitching your services, but as making a promise, a promise to solve people's problems and help them reach their goals. Unlike when you sell products, where the promise is immediately fulfilled, short-term success when selling your expertise comes from inspiring confidence that you can deliver on this promise. Long-term success comes from keeping your promise and exceeding expectations while also sourcing new business. Depending on your organization, you may be supported by a business development team of professional salespeople, which is great, but you want to be the one who determines the promise to the client because only you know the full extent of your capabilities.

When you choose *not* to sell, you limit your opportunities to apply the expertise you have worked so hard to build. You will be dependent on other people to sell your expertise, which is limited to their awareness of what you can do. Even if they understand the breadth of what you know *today*, they will not know the problems you can solve *tomorrow*. To land interesting work that is valuable to your professional growth, the success of your company, and your career opportunities, you want to be in front of your clients and adept at persuading them to engage you in ever more challenging work. When you take control of selling your abilities, you blaze your own growth path and actively prevent the professional stagnation that plagues those who do not sell.

When I use the term *sell*, I am referring to a process that entails much more than the simple, fleeting transaction of selling a product to a customer and moving on. Selling is not a task. When you're selling your expertise, you want to *develop* your business, a process that is ongoing and permanent. To develop something means to invest resources in building an *asset* that continues to create value. The three main assets you'll want to build as a rainmaker are your relationships, reputation, and expertise. Successful selling, like successful development, is about growing these assets over time. Accordingly, *selling* and *business development* are used interchangeably throughout the book.

Business development requires commitment. As author Pete Davis highlights in *Dedicated: The Case for Commitment in an Age of Infinite Browsing*, commitment has its own "momentum." He explains, "The more we commit to something, the more it opens up to us."[1] In the case of sales, by committing to generating revenue, we gain a deeper appreciation for it. Davis also points out that we psychologically adapt to the commitment we make:

> Everyone overestimates the psychological effects of change because we underestimate the power of our psychological immune system. Our psychological immune system works by weaving new stories out of our new circumstances. We start finding less meaning in what's outside of our control and new meaning in what's within our control.

When it comes to developing our business, this immune system allows us to focus on our sales activities, instead of whether or not we should be selling in the first place.

The point here is that once you commit to selling your expertise, and the work that comes along with it, you will find success. And that success will perpetuate further commitment to building up your book of business. In the process, business development will become an ongoing, critical part of your role, not just a phase or task to slog through. Think of the difference between "being on a diet" and "having a healthy diet"—one is an event, the other is a lifestyle. With any lifestyle change, the process can seem difficult, time consuming, and daunting. But once you're equipped with the right mindset, strategies, and tactics, you will find business development easier, and I daresay more enjoyable, creating a path to an even more meaningful professional career.

So, Why Should You Listen to Me?

Like many of you, I have spent much of my academic and professional career amassing expertise. After my failed stint as a Cutco salesperson, I graduated college with a double major in chemistry and economics and followed many of my classmates into financial services. I accepted a full-time position as an equities trader at a boutique proprietary trading firm, and I remember feeling so proud that my role did not involve soliciting clients—my sole responsibility was to make money using the firm's money. I developed expertise in capital markets, pattern recognition, and decision making, and I applied it to make profitable trades for my firm. In time, though, I found it wasn't for me.

Soon after, I moved to China to take a business management role at an international manufacturing firm. Upon returning to the US and reflecting on my career, I realized I had a passion for training and coaching. I landed a role at a health insurance company designing and facilitating training programs to build others' knowledge and skills. The only time I needed to "sell" was during the job interview. Beyond that, I focused on learning and doing the technical work. It wasn't until I joined Exec|Comm that I bore responsibility for generating revenue and that my sales number was seen as a major factor in assessing my performance and promotability. For the first time in my professional career, my success was heavily dependent upon my ability to bring in business, not my ability to put my technical expertise to work. (Technical work need not be "technical" in the traditional sense—in my case, my technical expertise is communication and business development skills training, instructional design, and executive coaching.) My selling muscles were severely underdeveloped, but I trained to get stronger, and I eventually was promoted to partner.

This is the book I wish I had read when I first started selling work. It's geared both toward people just beginning the process, who have little to no network, and established professionals who need a fresh injection of life into their book of business. To level the playing field for technically gifted doers, the material is designed as a tactical rainmaking manual. Early in my business development career, I had a theoretical sense of what sales was about and wasted both time and energy learning and applying sales tips and theories in a piecemeal way. I have personally used all of the advice presented, and I have found it to work for my clients and me. At the same time, I acknowledge that what works best for me may not work exactly the same for you. I hope to bridge this gap by sharing guiding principles rather than a do-it-exactly-this-way approach. I encourage you to pull out what is useful for you and judge the advice based on the results that you get.

My understanding of rainmaking comes from three perspectives: learner, practitioner, and teacher. As a continuous learner, I've culled academic research and practical tactics from hundreds of books and resources on rainmaking. As a practitioner with consistent results, the mindset, strategies, and tactics I suggest will help you prepare for, and overcome, the obstacles that often get in the way of building a successful book of business. From my experience as a corporate trainer, sales coach, and lecturer at Wharton, I've applied my teaching expertise to facilitate your learning, highlighting key principles and sharing a step-by-step approach to generate revenue. As a bonus, this book doesn't just leverage my insights; interviews with other successful rainmakers from a variety of professions and industries are peppered throughout, providing the type of advice that can only come from on-the-ground experience.[2] I also rely on the collective knowledge found in Exec|Comm's 40+ years of experience working with professionals from top accounting, law, and consulting firms, not to mention many Fortune 100 companies.

When it comes to driving revenue over time, we have found the following:

- Expertise alone is not enough.
- Enthusiasm alone is not enough.
- Experience alone is not enough.
- Intelligence alone is not enough.
- Strong relationships alone are not enough.
- Motivation alone is not enough.
- Likability alone is not enough.
- Luck alone is not enough.
- Optimism alone is not enough.
- Sales activity alone is not enough.

So, what is enough? An integrated mix of the rainmaking mindset, strategies, and tactics.

How This Book Is Organized

This book is organized into three major parts with multiple chapters, focusing on a tight integration of mindset, strategies, and tactics. Depending on your experience, you may feel more confident in one or two of these areas over the others. But to become a true rainmaker, all three need to be approached together: When you don't have the right mindset, you run the risk of alienating your clients or being held back by mental shackles. When you don't have the right strategies, you might be wasting your time on the wrong activities or pushing when you should be pulling. When you don't have the right tactics, you won't be able to execute on your strategy effectively.

Part I: Mindset. Part I explains how to adopt an effective mindset to set yourself up for rainmaking success. The way you perceive yourself and the world will heavily influence how you interpret your current situation and the actions you decide to take. The right mindset is therefore necessary before you develop and execute your sales strategy.

Part II: Strategies. Part II shifts focus from your mindset to the mindset of your prospects and clients. You'll learn concrete strategies to build your book of business and to match the right strategy to where your prospects are in the sales process. This section also includes practical metrics to help you measure your effectiveness in implementing those strategies. Whether you're in the early stages of researching clients you want to pursue, or the late stages of closing the deal, you'll find specific guidance to maximize your efforts.

Part III: Tactics. Part III teaches the key tactics to help you effectively execute on your strategies. You'll learn how to build a strong reputation to help you land more business, growing a network that provides value to both you and your contacts. By better understanding how to read the room in real-time and the nuances behind when to listen and when to talk, you can more effectively communicate and collaborate with your clients. Part III also gives advice on driving the sales process forward in a client-focused way, overcoming roadblocks that may arise. Most importantly, you'll leave with actionable ways to develop these skills and advice on staying relevant to ensure your success today and beyond.

In addition, "practical tips" sections are included in every chapter, highlighting an immediately useable piece of advice. Each chapter closes with reflection questions, metrics, or tactics to practice helping you apply what you learned to your own unique circumstances. All of the advice in the following pages is meant to help you generate revenue; improve your job and career opportunities; and build long-term client relationships. That may seem like a lot to promise, but once you start putting this advice to use, you will see results that can be replicated time and again. It all starts with the right mindset, so let's begin there.

Mindset

We typically think of our mindset as being just that: something *set* in place. Difficult to alter. Potentially unmovable. But to become successful rainmakers, we need to adopt the rainmaking mindset. We must see the world, our potential clients, and our value through the lens of a rainmaker. This often means changing the way we approach sales from the inside out, leaving behind any old assumptions or thought processes that may hold us back. Our mindset determines how we perceive the world, which influences our thoughts, actions, and habits. To start thinking like a rainmaker, you must first understand the rainmaker's mindset, compare it to your own, then figure out where the gaps are.

Research shows that to drive sustained change and growth, you must influence your self-concept—how you think about, evaluate, and perceive yourself.[1] So though assessing your mindset is important, it's only the beginning. Insights alone are not enough—you need to see yourself as a person who will apply those insights. Most people struggle with sales not because they can't learn sales skills, but because they don't see themselves as salespeople. They either subconsciously avoid selling, or they consciously tell themselves they cannot learn how to do it in the first place. Your willpower and determination to sell your expertise will heavily depend on your openness to see yourself as a rainmaker.

To start, challenge unhelpful but common assumptions about business development. If you equate selling with manipulating and exploiting others, you will likely struggle. No one wants to come across as callously pushing unneeded services, nor does anyone want to feel as if they are hassling or bothering potential clients. Instead, most people want to use their expertise to solve problems while maintaining a positive self-image.

The rainmaking mindset allows you to move beyond self-doubt and hesitance and get to work on building your book of business. When you adopt this mindset and enhance how you perceive yourself and the situation, you will find that your activities will become more purposeful and impactful. You will also spend less time debating whether or not you *should* sell and dedicate more time to actually selling.

Eagerly Dedicated

Chapter 1: Eagerly Dedicated

Many of you reading this book are already excited to start selling your expertise and services, but equally as many, if not more, cracked this book open with a skeptic's eye. Why? Because a lot of you, in all honesty, just don't want to sell. You probably believe the costs outweigh the benefits—selling is nebulous, time-consuming, and takes you away from the work you either love or are good at and find easy to do. Bringing in business is more difficult and less straightforward than delivering on engagements. Building a strong book of business requires that you win new clients, which often involves persuading people who don't know you well to hire you to solve their problems. That's not such a simple task, nor one most of us want to tackle.

You're smart. You're talented. For years, you've been honing your craft and taking pride in becoming an expert. The non-technical activities, like entertaining clients or networking, seem unimportant, and better left to people without "hard skills," or those who have the right personality and enjoy that type of work. Since you mainly deliver work, most of your client interactions are with people who already value your services. It may be easy to think that sales will naturally happen as you continue serving these clients and building up your reputation. Unfortunately, that limited vantage point is also why many people struggle to build their book of business.

To become a rainmaker, you first need the *desire* to bring in business. Fortunately, that motivation can be acquired and developed quite quickly once you fully understand the benefits of selling. Landing clients is the name of the game. You cannot generate increased revenue for your organization unless you are eager to sell and dedicated to succeeding, two hallmarks of any

5

professional rainmaker. To get there, you need to understand what may be dampening your enthusiasm for engaging in business development. If you are technically inclined, and pride yourself on solving complex problems, you may be prone to avoid selling for three reasons. By understanding these three reasons, and challenging the assumptions behind them, you will find yourself becoming more motivated to sell.

Why Smart People Struggle with Sales

Research shows that most people strongly resist any activity that threatens their status.[1] In many professional settings, there's a general distaste for sales for this exact reason: The role is typically not seen as glamorous or glorious, and people may feel as if selling is "beneath" them. That's why few, if any, professionals pursued a degree in "sales" at college or aspired to become a sales rep when they graduated. The typical sales job does not seem to require special qualifications or credentials. The compensation is often commission-based, and large companies hire tons of salespeople, making the bar to entry seem low. Further, to most people, a job always seems higher-status or more prestigious if they are not tasked to sell a service or product. Companies recognize these facts and rename job titles to mask the role. "Salesperson" becomes "consultant," "account executive," "solutions specialist," or any euphemism that hides the four-letter word *sell*.

Another reason smart people struggle with sales is that there is a lag time between effort and payoff. If you're a technical expert, you are likely accustomed to seeing your hard work directly translate into results. Whether you are modeling future cash flows or writing a brief, you know how long it will take to complete the task and what the end product will look like. As you shift more time and energy into business development, if you don't immediately see results, you may begin to question your approach and doubt your abilities. Worse yet, if you are compensated on the billable hours model, you may feel pressure to get back to billable work, considering your sales efforts unproductive and abandoning them.

The problem here is the sense of uncertainty that goes along with sales. Success for any given deal does not depend solely on the quality and quantity of your effort. Timing, buyer preferences, economic conditions, personal emergencies, and other factors outside of your control all impact whether you will close a deal. As a result, you may experience a strong pull toward non-selling activities that feel more like a "sure thing."

Senior managers in professional services firms often fall into this trap. Although it is clear that generating revenue is a critical step on the path to partnership, many professionals choose to spend the bulk of their time focusing on deepening their expertise, executing work already sold, managing teams, and improving internal best practices. These activities feel safer and more productive; they are well-defined, and you can immediately measure your results. Unfortunately, those tasks alone will not distinguish you at your firm and can hinder your career progression if not supplemented with strong revenue numbers.

The third reason smart people resist sales is because sales activity can appear—to be blunt—kind of boring. The tasks involved may come across as rote or intellectually dull. Maybe you got into your line of work because you like analyzing businesses, drafting contracts, or engineering financial solutions for your clients. You likely thrive on the intellectual stimulation of the work itself. The thought of replacing even a moment of that time for making X number of calls per month, or drafting multiple proposals that may go nowhere, seems out of synch with the work you know and enjoy. You didn't develop your expertise to let it just sit idle.

When these three reasons—perceived status downgrade, unproductive use of energy, and tediousness—come together, a full picture emerges of why so many professionals want to stay far, far away from sales. It boils down to two things: your satisfaction and your motivation. Research by organizational psychologists Richard Hackman and Greg Oldham identified five job characteristics that drive these two factors[2]:

1. **Skills Variety:** Performing tasks that are varied and challenging will be more motivating than carrying out routine and easy ones.

2. **Task Identity:** Being involved in an entire process and seeing the final result of your work will make that work more meaningful than if you'd only been involved in a sliver of the process.

3. **Task Significance:** Working on a task that positively impacts the lives of others will be more rewarding than a task that has a limited effect.

4. **Autonomy:** Having independence to decide how and when to complete your work will lead to greater job satisfaction than needing to follow a manual or a manager's specific instructions.

5. **Feedback:** Knowing whether you're doing the job well or not will be more motivating than not knowing where you stand.

Hackman and Oldham summarized the relationship between these five characteristics with the *Motivating Potential Score (MPS)*, which is used to predict how motivating a specific job might be. You'll see from the equation that autonomy and feedback are multipliers, which mean they play a more significant role in impacting satisfaction and motivation.

$$MPS = \frac{Skill\ Var + Task\ Id + Task\ Sig \times Autonomy \times Feedback}{3}$$

If you see sales as a status downgrade (low Task Significance), an unproductive use of energy (low Task Identity and Feedback), or tedious and boring (low Skill Variety), you are justified to focus your efforts elsewhere. Unfortunately, your decision would be misguided for both you and your organization since these three reasons rely on preconceived notions that, when examined, are false. They fail to account for the higher compensation, bigger titles, and increased autonomy that flow to individuals who can bring in business. Having a clear revenue target and having compensation tied directly to that number may be intimidating, but once you start experiencing sales success, they will be incredibly motivating. Your satisfaction is all but guaranteed as you begin to see the results on your own career.

Driving Revenue Leads to Growth

Although you may not aspire to sales, you probably do aspire to rise to the top levels of your firm. Your ability to drive revenue is paramount to achieving those goals. Nothing happens without revenue—you can't do the work until someone first sells it. Sales drives any firm: It turns on the lights and powers the coffee pot. It provides for employees' livelihoods and fuels investments for future growth. Without generating revenue, a business cannot exist.

As you well know, for most businesses, activities that increase profitability are usually considered more valuable. According to the simple profitability equation, Profits = Revenues − Costs, the value of your expertise is based on the revenue you generate, the costs you reduce, or both. The more revenue you can generate while keeping costs low, the more valuable you become. Firms see high revenue producers as valuable assets. As your client base grows and your revenue contribution increases, so will your opportunities and compensation. Conversely, when you don't bring in business, you run the risk of stunting both your growth and your earning potential.

For those of you with strong technical skills, you are probably well compensated. Unfortunately, from your organization's point of view, if you're only *delivering* work, you're on the cost side of the equation. For your firm to maintain its profitability, it is in their best interest to limit what they pay you. An investment banker who cannot source deals, a portfolio manager who cannot find investors, or a research analyst who cannot get clients to buy or trade on their research will hit a career ceiling. The same dynamic applies when you go in-house. If you do not directly bring in revenue, you'll need to continually justify your existence, while watching your back in case someone less costly arrives to take your place. The closer you get to directly generating profitable revenue, the more valuable you become. Your ability to sell will give you access to ever-increasing compensation, advancement, and job security. To that end, selling actually *enhances* your status.

As a professional with technical expertise, this idea may be hard to grasp. You likely calculate your value based on the depth of the expertise you have built over the years. It would stand to reason that the deeper your expertise, the more difficult it is to replicate, and the less likely it is that others will have the same skill set. This sense of scarcity may trick you into believing that doing something extremely difficult creates more value. But consider this idea in light of the profitability equation. The added effort to deepen your expertise is only valuable if it increases revenues and lowers costs—that's it. You can have all the expertise in the world, but if its added value isn't something a client will pay for, then it's not worth much, unfair as that might be. If you are unable to get clients to pay for your increased expertise, then you may be over-engineering your solutions or over-scoping your projects. You need to rethink your approach and readjust your place in the profitability equation.

The more revenue you generate, the more resources your organization will give you. With increased resources, you'll likely bring in even more revenue. This virtuous upward cycle is why being a rainmaker is a game-changer, as depicted in the cost-benefit analysis shown in Figure 1.1.

Rainmakers are not only well compensated, but they also experience a great deal of autonomy, which, as shown in the MPS equation, is highly motivating. Organizations understand that

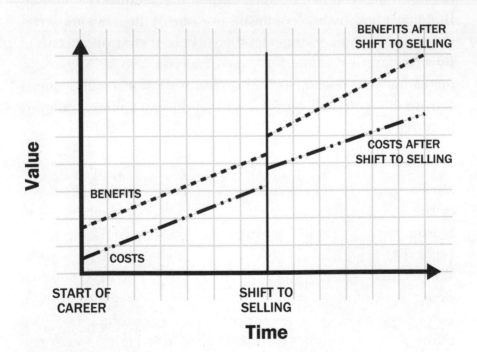

FIGURE 1.1 Actual Cost-Benefit Analysis of Selling Expertise

generating revenue involves many different and often time-intensive activities, and those organizations give their rainmakers plenty of latitude to be successful. As you integrate selling into your work, your professional growth, compensation, and autonomy increase, causing your benefit line, shown in Figure 1.1, to shift up, and become steeper.

If you have not generated revenue in the past, you will likely overestimate the difficulty of selling and the opportunity cost of shifting time away from your technical work. Although your cost line may shift up because of the added responsibility, the cost line will likely be flatter than you think. As you can see in Figure 1.1, because benefits rise more steeply than the costs once you start generating revenue, you'll want to get on the side of revenue as soon as possible.

Once you embrace the need to generate revenue for your organization, you've begun adopting the rainmaker mindset. Building a healthy book of business is one of the most impactful ways to contribute to the ongoing success of your organization. By bringing in revenue for your firm, you also help yourself, increasing your own opportunities for professional and financial growth. But you can't get there with enthusiasm alone. You need to turn pro.

Practical Tip

Assess right now whether your organization sees you on the side of revenue or cost. Ask yourself the following questions: Do you directly generate revenue for your firm? If so, how can you make revenue generation an even larger part of your role? If not, what can you do right now to bring in revenue for your firm?

True Professionals

Once you decide to get on the side of revenue, your path to becoming a rainmaker will be unique to you. That means you will need to figure out how *you* will succeed. It will be easy if you have family friends who happen to be executives at prospective clients, or if your firm has such a strong reputation, you are awash in high-quality leads. It will also help if you have more time than the rest of us, better technology than your competitors, and you work in a healthier economy than most. If you actually have these elements going for you, you have a great head start.

More often than not, though, you won't have any of these advantages; you'll have to work just as hard as, if not harder than the next person. Like all other rainmakers-to-be, you will face challenges, setbacks, and obstacles. Your success will depend in large part on taking ownership of your circumstances and learning to succeed despite the many roadblocks along the way. American Author Robert Louis Stevenson echoed this sentiment when he said, "Life is not a matter of holding good cards but playing a poor hand well."[3]

As a rainmaker, figuring out how to hit your revenue targets is your job—not your firm's. No one will force you to reach out to prospects. No one will tell you how to build your business. But at the end of the year, you either hit your revenue numbers, or you didn't. And you'll be the only one who knows if you gave it all you had or not. In many ways, your business development results are on you. Even when that may not feel like the case, your best bet is to take complete ownership of your situation and act as if no one is coming to your rescue.

Accepting total responsibility for your results empowers you to productively channel your energy. An unproductive use of energy might include complaining about what you don't have, blaming others for not providing adequate support, or making excuses about why you didn't hit your revenue target. Instead, that energy should be re-purposed, as you take responsibility to focus on what you can control: *becoming better*. When you hit your goals, you receive recognition and financial rewards. When you miss them, you learn where you went wrong and what you could have done better. Mistakes will be made, and you'll need to accept them. But persistence is key. If you're not willing to dedicate the time, do the work, and own the outcome of your efforts, then you'll never truly become a professional rainmaker.

From Amateur to Pro

Senior accounting partners and investment banking MDs often engage my firm to help build up the business development skills of their junior partners and mid-level bankers and instill a sense of ownership around sourcing business. They feel their people are only dabbling in business development, not fully owning it as an essential part of their role. A team member might squeeze in a networking event here, a follow-up call to an old client there, or an email to a new contact when they happen to think of it. If billable client work picks up, team members may go weeks—sometimes months—without performing any business development activities.

Dabbling is not uncommon when professionals first start developing business. They are given little advice or tools to work with, and many feel as if they've been thrown into the ocean without a life raft. A former investment banker who is now the Head of Strategy at a Fortune 500 firm recalled having such an experience during his first forays into business development. His senior colleagues advised him to build a relationship with the CFO from one of their deals by "hanging around the hoop and letting people warm up to you." That was the full guidance he received. He tried to foster a relationship, calling the CFO from time to time to "check-in," but he rarely had anything particular or useful to discuss. He found these check-ins awkward and a waste of time for both him and the CFO. He thought to himself, "This is not going to go anywhere. They already have a banker they are working with." He then turned his attention back to building up his deal list and resumé instead of developing executive-level relationships. Though he understood the importance of bringing in revenue, he was unable, or perhaps unwilling, to shift his mindset toward that of a professional rainmaker.

Every workday, your mental attention is pulled in seemingly endless directions. You're constantly deciding where to invest your time to get the best ROI. Like most people, you probably focus your energy at work on one of two activities: the one you view as your main function or the one you enjoy the most. If business development doesn't fall into either of those buckets, you'll struggle to put more energy there. To be a rainmaker, you need to make business development your main function. When you don't put a significant emphasis on your business development activities, you're essentially committing to remain an amateur. In *The War of Art*, author Steven Pressfield articulates the difference between amateurs and professionals as such: "An amateur has amateur habits. A professional has professional habits."[4] Can it really be that simple? Well, in a way, yes. In the context of rainmaking, it's easy to see where you stand. As you read the following, assess which side you're on, that of the amateur or the pro, and consider what you need to do to make the leap from one side to the other.

Professionals Show Up

Amateurs show up only when they feel inspired. They need motivation, inspiration, or aspiration to reach out to clients and develop their book of business. Even when they do show up, they work in bursts and often take breaks, such as reaching out to five clients one week and none the week after. Professional rainmakers show up *every day*, even if they don't feel inspired. They understand the importance of daily business development activities and work diligently.

Professionals Chop Wood

Amateurs focus on the rewards, fantasizing about what they will do with their bonus once they land a sizeable deal or a marquee client. After a big win, they may choose to reward themselves with a break from business development. Professional rainmakers concentrate on their activities, which are within their control, figuring out how to achieve their goals rather than what they will gain. When professional rainmakers experience success, they acknowledge it, and then go right back to work. For some, the win fuels even more sales activity.

Professionals Don't Make Excuses

Amateurs lean on excuses, whether legitimate or illegitimate. They make statements like, "I've been meaning to reach out. . ., "It's been a crazy week. . .," or "I know I should have done this but. . . ." Professional rainmakers find a way to get the work done even if something unexpected happens. They figure out how to make up for lost time, bad luck, or fatigue, and they plan for the unexpected. They recognize that just because they had a good reason for failing to meet their commitments, in the end, they still didn't meet them.

Professionals Keep Trying

Amateurs stall when they fail. When they've reached out to a potential buyer but have nothing to show for the attempted engagement, they say, "Sorry. They didn't respond to my email.

Not much else I could do." Professional rainmakers understand that you only fail if you stop trying. They say, "I couldn't reach them by email. I just tried pinging my friend, who also works at the company, to see if they can introduce me. Let me check on LinkedIn. . ."

Professionals Measure Their Performance

When building skills, amateurs rarely measure their progress against a performance benchmark. They are usually inconsistent in their performance and trailing the pack. They miss revenue milestones and do the bare minimum when it comes to activity metrics. Professional rainmakers track their progress and create deadlines to hit high performance standards. They ramp up the activity when they are behind their goal and do everything they can to meet their revenue commitments.

You'll notice that throughout this section, the word "amateur" has been used, but not the phrase "amateur rainmaker." The fact of the matter is that there are no *amateur* rainmakers. You're either a rainmaker or you're not—being a professional comes with the territory. As Roger Kneebone, a former surgeon turned researcher on experts, states in his book *Expert: Understanding the Path to Mastery*, "As a professional, even your *worst* performance needs to be good enough."[5] Professional rainmakers always deliver.

The good news is, no matter where you currently stand, *you can turn pro right now*. You don't need permission. You don't need a certification. You don't need someone else's blessing. To become a professional rainmaker, you need to commit yourself to showing up and working on your business development plan every day—no excuses. You'll have to figure out what you need to do to move sales conversations forward and drive your revenue numbers up. When you get stuck, you have to take responsibility to get unstuck, instead of depending on others to figure it out. No one can do your push-ups for you. To get stronger, you need to put in the work.

Turning pro means you're committing to win. In professional services, when you don't win, you don't see the payoff. Much of the work you put in to get your clients interested in a deal goes to waste when they don't follow through on it. Even after you turn pro, you'll want to be vigilant to stay pro. If you're not careful, it's always easier to fall back into amateur behaviors. Recognizing the outsized benefits of generating business will help you avoid this pitfall. The right mindset naturally leads to the right habits to help you better execute your business development strategies and tactics. Though it may be intimidating at first, dedicating yourself to building your book of business and following that desire to sell will open up a whole new world for you. You'll be squarely on the side of revenue and on your way to becoming a rainmaker.

Self-Reflection Questions

1. What beliefs do I have about selling that may dampen my desire to sell?

2. What roadblocks may prevent me from shifting from only delivering work to delivering *and* selling work?

3. Am I on the revenue side or the cost side at my firm? How close am I to directly generating revenue for my organization?

4. Why do I want to sell? What benefits will it bring to me? How are rainmakers at my organization treated?

5. What habits can I cultivate today to turn pro?

CHAPTER
2

Authentically Open

Chapter 2: Authentically Open

Whether you realize it or not, you've been selling all your life. For decades you've convinced, persuaded, and influenced other people to make an exchange of some sort—increase your allowance, agree to a date, hire you for an internship, get staffed on that exciting new account. Any time you ask someone to give you their time, energy, attention, or money, you are selling. You've been honing your sales skills for a long time already; now, you need to turn them toward selling the work you've been delivering so well.

"Yes," you might say, "but that's different. I don't know if I can sell my expertise. I'm just not a *salesperson*." Rainmaking is itself an expertise. As the late K. Anders Ericsson, renowned professor of human performance, reminds us, "Consistently and overwhelmingly, the evidence showed that *experts are always made, not born*."[1] As an extension, rainmakers are always made, not born. Think about how much time and effort you've put into your chosen profession to get where you are today. Learning how to sell is certainly no harder than the technical expertise you have built. One of my colleagues is a former attorney. He routinely tells law firm partners he coaches, "I've been a lawyer and I've been a salesperson. Being a lawyer is harder. It takes more discipline, diligence, and more attention to detail. Between sales and lawyering, you're already doing the harder job."

When it comes to rainmaking, though, our default mindset is often defeatist—we just aren't sure if we'll ever make it. As my colleague says, "Sales is just harder on the ego. You can be a good lawyer all day long and no one outright rejects you. But when you pitch to a new client and they go with another firm, it stings." Uncertainty abounds, along with a fear of failure, so we hedge

21

our efforts and close ourselves off to opportunities right in front of us. In so doing, we subconsciously sabotage ourselves, when we should be encouraging ourselves. You need to move beyond any limiting beliefs and stay open to the real possibility that you *will* become a rainmaker.

Growth Mindset and Self-Efficacy

Stanford Psychology Professor Carol Dweck spent decades studying people's beliefs about their own intelligence, talents, and abilities. According to her book, *Mindset: Changing the Way You Think to Fulfill Your Potential*,[2] you either see these qualities as unchangeable, meaning you have a "fixed mindset," or adjustable, in which case you have a "growth mindset." People with a fixed mindset see themselves as a finished product and interpret every challenge as a test of their abilities. For them, success at a particular task confirms their natural talent; failure painfully confirms their incompetence at the task at hand. People with a fixed mindset use statements such as "I'm not good with numbers" or "I'm not a people person." Dweck's research[3] shows that such individuals shy away from challenging opportunities because these situations increase the likelihood of failure. Instead, these people usually choose to stay in their comfort zone, reinforcing their sense of competence.

On the other hand, people with growth mindsets think of themselves as works in progress, and they view challenges as an opportunity to further develop their skills. Success at a task affirms their efforts; failure at a task leads to insights for learning. Their growth mindset naturally pushes them to seek out more challenging problems as a path for self-improvement.

Reflect on an instance when you received constructive feedback in a mid-year review. Did you interpret the critique as an indictment of your talent or as instructions for improvement? If you responded defensively or argued with the criticism, maybe even trying to undermine the person sharing the feedback, you likely lean toward a fixed mindset. If you decided to invest more time and effort to turn your performance around, you tend toward a growth mindset. The growth mindset allows rainmakers to overcome challenges and learn from their mistakes during the sales process. It helps them move forward and persist in the face of rejection (as discussed in Chapter 4). But even if you find yourself trapped in a fixed mindset more often than not, know that a growth mindset can be cultivated.[4]

In addition to Dweck's research, studies strongly show that an important factor to learning sales is self-efficacy, the belief that *you can and will* learn the skill.[5] High self-efficacy facilitates learning because it influences you to take on more challenging scenarios, put more effort into the process, and focus on learning, as opposed to performing. It's the difference between saying, "I can't do that," and "I don't know how to do that yet." Research has shown that training targeted at improving your self-efficacy around, for example, learning negotiation skills, will make you a better negotiator.[6] In other words, *believing* you can or can't becomes a self-fulfilling prophecy.

A practical way to begin developing a growth mindset is to see yourself as *a learner* rather than *a performer*. Performers look to *get things right*. Learners focus on *improving their abilities*. In a sales context, when a deal falls through, a performer gets disappointed, while a learner becomes curious. When you don't win a particular deal, instead of beating yourself up, reflect on what you can learn to increase your chances of closing the next deal. Think back to any recurring objections from your prospects in pitches you have made over the last year. Or, better yet, ask your close contacts at those companies for feedback on what you could have done differently.

To assess your shift to a growth mindset, monitor how you interpret your abilities. Ideally, you want to move from "I'm not good with numbers," to "I need more practice reading financial statements," or from "I'm not a people-person," to "I need to put more effort into building rapport." Of course, it's not just about learning—your performance and results matter. The ultimate measure of your sales success will be the amount of profitable revenue you bring into your firm. Although you might experience the occasional "lucky break" or unfortunate setback, over the long run, the revenue you generate will reflect your skill level. Still, it can sometimes be hard to untangle skill from luck, and the combination can lead us astray.

Practical Tip

In most cases, when it comes to business development skills or activities, there is no such thing as *can't*. If you catch yourself saying "can't," replace it with "don't know how," "don't want to," or "don't believe I can." For example, "I can't reach the decision-maker," becomes "I don't know how to reach the decision-maker yet. Let me figure it out."

The Skill-Luck Combo

The amount of revenue you generate is influenced by both skill and luck. Skill is the ability to apply your expertise to achieve a specific outcome. Luck consists of the factors beyond your control that can help or hurt you in achieving your outcome. In his book, *The Success Equation: Untangling Skill and Luck in Business, Sports, and Investing*, Michael Mauboussin, Investment Strategist and Adjunct Professor at Columbia Business School, introduces the skill-luck continuum. On one end are games of skill. On the other end are games of chance. To test whether an activity involves skill, the simple question to ask yourself is, "Can I lose on purpose?"[7] If you can intentionally lose, by choosing to do nothing or by doing something incorrectly, then the activity involves skill.

Both technical work and rainmaking, by Mauboussin's definition, involve skill. The difference between the two is where they lie on the skill-luck continuum. Technical work is closer to the skill side, and rainmaking is closer to the luck side, as shown in Figure 2.1.

When you perform your technical work, you have a high certainty that you can apply your expertise and get the results you want. When you sell, there are more variables that lie beyond your control. For example, your success in landing a client engagement is dependent not only on your individual performance throughout the sales interaction, but also on the timing of those interactions, the mood of the decision-makers, the state of the economy, and the reaction of your competitors, just to name a few. When luck is involved, you might do all the right activities and still not close a sale. Alternatively, you might land the deal despite a weak sales strategy and approach.

Think of technical work like playing chess and business development like playing poker. In chess, if you make the right moves, you will likely win the game. In poker, you can do everything right and still lose due to luck, but you can minimize

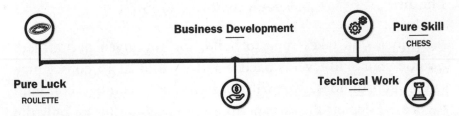

FIGURE 2.1 Technical Work and Business Development on the Skill-Luck Continuum

the impact of luck by maximizing your level of skill. The same is true in business development.

How Luck Derails Your Ability to Become a Rainmaker

If you've already begun your business development efforts, you've likely noticed that some of your peers seem to get off to a fast start, while others languish. It can be frustrating when you work extra hours to squeeze sales activities into your day and see little progress, while others seem to find success despite minimal effort. It's hard not to feel deflated, discouraged, and demotivated when your actions don't seem to matter or lead to the results you want.[8] This despondency hurts your chances of success. You may question your ability to learn sales (your self-efficacy), and then stop engaging in certain sales activities—even the right ones—because you believe they are ineffective. What you may not realize is that this inconsistency in sales outcomes, especially if you're following an effective process, is normal, and not an indication that you're doing anything wrong.

To help you see how sales performance is impacted by the combination of skill and luck more clearly, consider the following example comparing the results of a beginner (Skill = 2) and the results of a rainmaker (Skill = 8). To keep it simple, let's say you are considered a rainmaker when your average sales performance (the sum of skill and luck) is above a rating of 10:

$$Rainmaker = (Skill + Luck) > 10$$

Since skill takes time to build, for any given period, let's assume your skill level is fixed. So, if we look at 15 consecutive sales opportunities, we will hold the skill number constant. Figure 2.2 depicts the sales performance accounting for only the skill component.

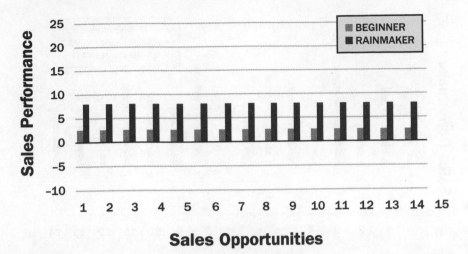

FIGURE 2.2 Beginner vs. Rainmaker Sales Performance over 15 Consecutive Opportunities (Skill Only)

Luck, by definition, is out of our control and unpredictable, so we won't know how much of it we will get, and in which direction (good or bad). For this thought exercise, luck will be the same for each opportunity for both the beginner and the rainmaker. The numbers representing luck have been randomly chosen between –15 and +15 for each sales opportunity. When comparing the results of a beginner to the results of a seasoned rainmaker for the same set of opportunities, the impact of skill and luck on sales performance is clear. The average sales performance for a rainmaker is above 10; for a beginner, it is above 5, given the same amount of luck for each person (see Figure 2.3).

At a lower skill level, luck has a more significant impact on your performance. Even if your skill level is low, you can still win opportunities because of the luck component. Conversely, even experienced rainmakers can lose deals if they are unlucky. But if you increase your skill, your average sales performance *will* rise. This dynamic may make sales feel somewhat random at first, but

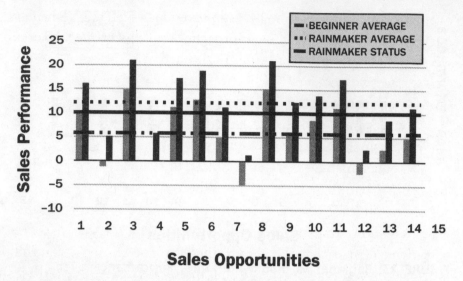

FIGURE 2.3 Beginner vs. Rainmaker Sales Performance over 15 Consecutive Opportunities (Skill and Luck)

if you focus on pushing your skill level higher, and keep increasing the number of sales opportunities you pursue, the results will come.

Luck can also distort how we perceive our sales skills. Sometimes, we are just in the right place at the right time. When a client reaches out to you with a need that results in business, you may believe you made the sale because of the way you handled the sales interactions. In reality, the deal may have closed because your client's situation was so urgent, they chose the first person who responded to their request. (Aren't you glad you didn't take that day off?) If we're not careful, lucky wins can make us prone to two biases that can derail our learning: the *self-serving bias*,[9] the tendency to attribute our success to skill and failure to bad luck, and the *outcome bias*,[10] our tendency to judge the quality of a decision based on the results.

When we take more credit than we deserve for our sales wins and blame other factors for our losses (self-serving bias), we overestimate our abilities to bring in revenue, which may dampen our interest in learning new approaches and techniques. When we misjudge the merit of certain sales activities because we tie the results we received with the effectiveness of the activity (outcome bias), we risk repeating activities that won't help us generate revenue or ceasing activities that are productive for landing business. Guard against these two biases.

As you start building your book of business, remember that no matter what happens with your sales results in the short term, a higher skill level is what will help you succeed in the long run. Research shows that any time there is extreme luck, either good or bad, performance will revert to the average.[11] As in poker, the more hands you play, the more skill matters. To further increase your chances of becoming a rainmaker, you'll want to leverage your strengths, and be aware of your blind spots when developing business. To help you get used to sales being your primary function, you'll also want to make sure you feel genuine about the way you sell. This authenticity can only come from first understanding who you are.

Know Who You Are

When you're new to business development, you may feel tremendous pressure to emulate someone else. You may even feel you need to become someone you're not in order to succeed. You will likely get advice to do *this*, be like *that*, act more like *this person*. Although this advice might be well-intentioned, it can be distracting and misguided. What works for others may not work for you. For example, many people believe that effective salespeople are extroverts, since the role requires you to connect with people you don't know. When Wharton Professor Adam Grant studied this assumption, his research showed a "weak and conflicting relationship between extraversion and sales performance."[12] There is no one successful archetype to rainmaking. To succeed, you want to develop business in a way that is *authentically* you.

Tom Liu, Managing Director at Bank of America Securities, has seen this fact play out throughout his career. Liu started shifting from delivering work to selling work early on, as he realized generating revenue was key to promotions and further success. He spent much of his time shadowing other rainmakers. He recounts, "Once you observe others, you find that there is really no one way of selling. There are multiple ways of selling, and watching others gives you different options to consider." He points out that "at the end of the day, you have to know yourself. You have to adopt the style that works for you. You can't be someone that you're not. You need to be comfortable with the way you sell."

What will differentiate you with clients is likely not *what* problems you're able to solve but *how* you solve those problems. By finding your voice and unique way of working, you'll build more genuine, trusting relationships. When asked his recommendation for successfully sourcing and closing deals in investment banking, without hesitation, Liu says, "Know yourself. Know what you are comfortable with. Know what you are able to do. Know your limitations." In his case, when Liu is selling his expertise, he speaks to the specific value he can provide his potential clients. "For me, that comes from my technical background, which is substantive, so I use that as a tool to sell. To bring value to my clients, I'll hit on complex technical issues and solutions, versus saying, 'Hey, hire me because I'm here for you' or 'hire me because I'm the lowest cost.'" For Liu, knowing who he is and developing his own style always seemed straightforward, but he recognizes that for many aspiring rainmakers, this might not be so easy.

Since we have a front-row seat to our lives, we might think we know ourselves well. Why wouldn't we? We've been living with ourselves all our lives. Surprisingly, according to survey data, "95% of people believe they are self-aware, but the real number is 12 to 15 percent."[13] This gap in self-awareness likely stems from the following:

- We can easily recall many of our life events, but we rarely reflect on how they've shaped our belief systems, or revealed our natural talents, personality, and interests.
- We have difficulty discerning between who we are and who we think we should be.
- We haven't given much thought to who we truly are.

Part of becoming a rainmaker comes from enhancing your self-awareness so you can leverage your most unique quality—*you*. Start by collecting data points about yourself through a self-inventory. To warm up, consider "above the surface" traits, like educational background, professional experience, and demographics. List out these facts about yourself. For instance, for my "above the surface" traits, I'd include the following:

- I majored in chemistry and economics.
- I have an MBA.
- I have experience working in financial services, manu-facturing, healthcare, and academia.
- I've been a researcher, an equities trader, a business owner, and a teacher.
- I'm of Chinese heritage, was born in Hong Kong, and was raised in the US.
- I'm a husband and a parent of two kids.

Now, move on to the "below the surface" qualities: your core values, strengths and limitations, personality and worldview, and interests. Unless you're highly self-aware, or have devoted time to reflect on these qualities, they are likely less clear to you than your "above the surface" traits. To help you think about these qualities, consider the following:

- **Core Values:** Our values guide what we think, say, and do. They serve as a compass to help us navigate our experiences and guide our daily decisions. Aligning our actions with our values will help us feel authentic and consistent. To heighten the awareness of your value system, look closely at how you spend your money, time, and effort. You can also reflect on the criteria you've used in the past to make important personal and professional decisions. Knowing your values will help you decide which clients to take on and which to pass up, or the ways you'll best connect and work with your clients.

- **Strengths and Limitations:** Since our strengths come easily to us, we mistakenly believe they come easily to everyone. When we don't recognize our strengths, we may not actively nurture or develop them. You can take an assessment to help uncover your top strengths—such as the VIA Character Strengths Survey[14] and the CliftonStrengths assessment[15]—but you can also just observe your day-to-day interactions. Note the tasks people ask you to help them with or the topics you often teach others. What comes easily to you that others seem to struggle with? Ask people who know you well what they see as your strengths—and limitations. Your performance reviews at work may offer additional insights.

- **Personality and Worldview:** Our personality and worldview are shaped by a combination of our genetic makeup and life experiences; they impact how we interact with, and react to, the world. Despite controversy[16] surrounding personality assessments, and though they don't provide the "truth" of who we are, the results can still help enhance our business development efforts. For example, if you knew you had a high-level of agreeableness, you may want to learn how to say "no" to requests that take you away from your business development time. Popular assessments include the Big 5 Personality Profile (OCEAN), Myers-Briggs Type Indicator (MBTI), and The Enneagram. Your organization may have access to these types of assessments, so check in with your HR department. There are also free versions online.[17]

- **Interests:** We rarely need motivation when we engage in activities that interest us. If you can plug into an activity related to selling that doesn't require external motivation, you will "outwork" others who may not have the same interests. To better recognize your interests, think about what functions you enjoy performing most at work, what activities you gravitate toward during your spare time, and what subjects captivate your attention. Your responses may influence what industry you decide to focus on, what type of clients you pursue, and how you approach the sales process as a whole.

Both above the surface and below the surface data are important in helping you recognize how you can bring your background, personality, values, and interests to bear on your business development approach.

Bring Who You Are to the Table

As you reflect on who you are, consider how you can use your unique attributes to better serve your clients. What are you able and willing to do that others can't, won't, or don't? Perhaps you are ultra-responsive and can follow up with more clients due to your process-orientation and penchant for productivity systems. Maybe you shine at networking events because you can meaningfully connect with anyone, or you've gone above and beyond on certain projects because they align with your values. No matter what they are, leverage your strengths and interests when building your book of business. For example:

- If you're gifted at writing, and not as comfortable speaking in public, find ways to get published instead of trying to land speaking engagements.

- If you make a stronger impression when meeting people face to face, spend more time at conferences and other live events.

- If you enjoy traveling and learning about different cultures, you might look to work with multinational organizations that will value your cultural awareness.

Don't confuse being yourself with being stuck in your ways. If you're not already a rainmaker, you'll need to stretch outside of your comfort zone to transition from being *you* to becoming the *rainmaker you*.

Harvard Business School Professor Herminia Ibarra studied management consultants and investment bankers as they transitioned from technical work to become trusted advisors to clients. She noted that this transition involved three steps. The participants would (1) observe different role models in action, (2) experiment with adopting the behaviors observed, and

(3) evaluate the experience against the success of the approach and the participant's comfort level.[18] Their evaluation helped them to decide whether the approach was worth keeping.

Some of the research participants fully imitated their role models, while others hesitated to emulate them because they wanted to stay true to themselves. The study showed that those who were hesitant to try a different approach hurt their transition from technical work to managing client relationships. Ibarra found that the participants best able to navigate this transition were open to "trying" on different behaviors. According to Ibarra, refusing to step out of our comfort zone in an effort to "stay true to who we are" can potentially hold us back. She reminds us, "Because doing things that don't come naturally to you can make you feel like an impostor, authenticity easily becomes an excuse for staying in your comfort zone. The trick is to work toward a future version of your authentic self by doing just the opposite: stretching way outside the boundaries of who you are today."[19]

Simply put, to think like a rainmaker, you need to act like a rainmaker. Then, as you reflect on your behaviors, you'll find yourself stepping into the mindset of a rainmaker. Some might call this idea "faking it until you make it." If you find that phrase distasteful, replace "faking it" with "experimenting with potential future selves" (not as catchy, but we all need a good euphemism every now and then to get through the day). Once you find a future self that helps you achieve your next-level goals, you assimilate it into your identity. This constant experimentation is essentially an evolutionary process. The next time you feel inauthentic trying a new approach, remember that it's part of your evolution. Give it time so you can better decide whether to incorporate these new behaviors as part of who you are. As you lean into being authentic while staying openminded, you'll begin to build relationships *your* way. Sell *your* way. Take care of clients *your* way. In doing so, you'll attract clients who value your unique qualities. They'll appreciate what you bring to the table, and by being authentically you and open to growth, you'll further increase your probability of success.

Self-Reflection Questions

1. Do I have a fixed mindset or growth mindset? What are two things I can do today to move toward cultivating a growth mindset?

2. When I am learning something new, how often am I performing as opposed to learning? In my last sales interaction, did I focus on performing or learning?

3. How have luck and skill impacted my business development results so far? Have I confused the two, and if so, how has that affected my performance?

4. How have the self-serving bias and outcome bias impacted my thinking? What is one example of this in my real-life?

5. How can I use my core values, strengths and limitations, personality and worldview, and interests to develop business, build relationships, and serve my clients?

6. What is one action I can take to "try on" a rainmaker behavior?

3

Consistently Client-Focused

Chapter 3: Consistently Client-Focused

A common misperception about gifted rainmakers is that they can sell anything to anyone. Whether the proverbial ice to Alaskan Inuits or a pen to a random person on the street, the subtext is that talented salespeople trick us into paying for things we don't need. Many professionals avoid selling because they feel like it involves manipulating or misleading others. They believe they are doing something *to* someone as opposed to *for* someone. When mid-level professionals reach the point in their careers when they are first encouraged to sell, they often feel uneasy and disingenuous. I regularly hear some variation of, "I never had problems connecting with people at social events and conferences, but now I'm uncomfortable talking to people in those settings because, in my mind, I feel like I'm constantly looking for an angle to sell them something. It's no longer a conversation. It feels completely inauthentic."

The best conversations are those in which we truly bond with the other person. Whether we're chatting about recent events, our plans for the future, personal issues, or any topic in between, when we remain present, attentive, and engaged, we find a way to connect in a natural, unforced way. But when we shift to business development, it seems like these topics might all go out the window. As we feel pressure to find leads and "make something happen," we begin to force connections and conversations, even pitching our services when it's clearly not the right time or place. We focus on getting something from the other person, and often, that person senses this intent and finds it off-putting. Rainmakers, however, persuade by remaining genuinely focused on *the other person's needs*, helping them recognize opportunities to better achieve their goals.

Mohamed Kande, Global Advisory Leader for PwC, a global professional services organization, echoes this sentiment:

> "The secret is actually not about selling. It's never about selling. It's about helping people and companies understand and solve the challenges they face. It always starts with the person on the other side. You're not selling your services to them; you're helping them buy what they need to solve their problems."

Don't sell—help buy. Clients buy your services when they have a real issue that would be best be solved by paying you to solve it. Instead of thinking about how to sell someone your services, you need to think of how you can resolve their problems using your expertise. You must remain focused on them, not on you. A large part of your success in selling work will come from building enough trust so your clients actually share their needs, allowing you in to help them. Your clients must see you not as a *seller*, but as an *assistant buyer*.

Become an Assistant Buyer through Trust

Think of the last time you made a big purchase. Maybe it was a car, a house, or a graduate education. You likely enlisted several people to help you: a close friend, a trusted real estate agent, or one of your favorite professors. You chose these people because you felt they had your best interest in mind and their experience and expertise were relevant to your situation. Basically, you *trusted* them. To become an assistant buyer, you need your clients to trust you.

Research from Princeton Professor Susan Fiske and her colleagues has found that we trust people based on our perception of their warmth and competence. Whenever we meet someone, we intuitively ask ourselves two questions, one related to warmth and the other to competence: first, and crucially, "Does this person or group intend to harm or help me?"

Second, "Does this person or group have the ability to enact those intentions?"[1] When new prospects meet with you in an initial business development interaction, they ask themselves the same questions. Since it's hard for them to know whether you truly want to help or you just want their money, you will initially be viewed as a potential threat. Only after your prospects believe you are there to help—and can help—will they evaluate whether to do business with you.

According to Fiske's research, most high-end advisors, such as lawyers, accountants, and bankers, are perceived to have high competence and below-average warmth.[2] What often exacerbates this dynamic is the tendency for these professionals to lead with their credentials—focusing on themselves—as compared to leading with warmth, which shows their clients or prospects they're there for them. Take a moment and think of someone with whom you work closely. Next, using the Warmth vs. Competence Criteria in Table 3.1, decide whether they exhibit low or high warmth and low or high competence.

Table 3.1 Warmth vs. Competence Criteria

Low Warmth	High Warmth
• Doesn't seem to consider the needs and goals of others	• Shows consideration for the needs and goals of others
• Projects arrogance and leads with talking	• Projects humility and leads with listening
• Comes across as unapproachable and closed off	• Comes across personable, sincere, and kind
• Breaks confidences, dismisses others, and creates an unsafe and exclusive environment	• Keeps confidences, remains non-judgmental, and creates a safe and inclusive environment

(continued)

(continued)

Low Competence	High Competence
• Has a weak reputation and few references	• Has a strong reputation and credible references
• Displays spotty track record with no sign of career advancement or achievements	• Possesses notable credentials and achievements and quick career progression
• Unable to accomplish goals and seems unreliable	• Demonstrates strong execution, responsiveness, and follow through
• Speaks nervously and appears unsure and unprepared	• Speaks with certitude and appears confident

Now for the hard part: How do you think others typically perceive you when it comes to warmth and competence? Based on your self-assessment, try plotting yourself on the warmth-versus-competence quadrants in Figure 3.1.

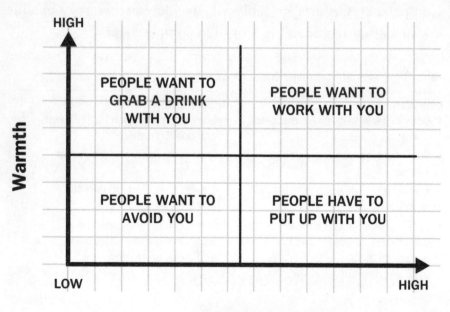

FIGURE 3.1 Warmth vs. Competence Quadrants

Of course, warmth alone won't be enough. As shown in the figure, if potential clients deem you high in warmth but low in competence, they might grab a coffee or drink with you but not hire or refer you. If they decide you are high in competence but low in warmth, they may respect you, and they might be willing to hire you—as long as they don't have to interact with you.[3] (Given the competitive nature of most professional services work, however, we need our clients and prospects to *want to* work with us, not just *be resigned* to working with us.) If they judge you to be low in both dimensions, they will find a way to politely exit the interaction. From a rainmaking standpoint, your goal is to continually maximize both your warmth and competence to gain your prospects' or clients' trust.

No matter what dimension you need to develop (warmth or competence), the endgame is to focus on your client. Even the definitions of warmth and competence will depend on your clients' preferences and background. You may have one client who requires a certain pedigree or level of education, and another who may be wary of too many letters after your name. In some cultures, strong eye contact shows confidence, but in others, it might be seen as disrespectful. The point is you must decrease your self-orientation and increase your client-orientation. This mindset shift to focus less on yourself and more on others will transform the way you interact with your prospects and clients.

Practical Tip

Open up an email you recently sent to a client and count up the number of "you" and "yours" versus "I," "me," and "my." To help you shift your mindset to focus more on your client, consider reframing some of your sentences to increase the reference to your reader rather than yourself. One way to do that is to convert "I," "me," and "my" to "you" and "yours."

Focus Less on Yourself and More on Others

When you stay focused on the needs of others, what you say, and how you say it will begin to shift naturally. You'll start to connect the message you want to convey with why the other person you're speaking to should care. When selling, this client orientation enhances your relevance to potential buyers, and according to research, it leads to deeper trust on their part and greater job satisfaction on yours.[4] To boost trust by focusing more on others, consider adopting the following five behaviors.

1. Put the Spotlight on Others

One way to assess how "others-focused" you are is to monitor how much airtime you take up in an interaction. Mohamed Kande of PwC explains, "When clients want to buy something, they want to understand how you will address their needs and what they are going to get. . . So, stop talking about yourself. Just talk about them." By focusing a conversation on your clients, and letting them speak most of the time, you automatically guide the discussion toward your clients' objectives and concerns (as explored further in Chapter 10). Remember, your client is not there to help you generate more revenue for your firm. They are there to explore whether or not you can either solve their problem or help them take advantage of an opportunity. To keep the spotlight on them, demonstrate curiosity.

Curiosity comes from accepting that there is much you don't know, paired with the sincere desire to keep learning. To help you tap into your natural curiosity, think about all the aspects you don't know about your prospects, their business, their lives, and their aspirations. Consider their background, professionally and culturally. Learn what you can about them before reaching out to better understand where they are coming from and how to best interact with them. When you speak with them, if you leave the conversation without having learned something new, you were likely not curious enough.

As you learn more about your clients' preferred way of working, you'll want to *actively demonstrate* your recognition of those preferences. This emphasis will look different depending on your client's communication style. For example, with clients who are action-oriented and results-driven, shorten the rapport building upfront. Cover your key points directly and move quickly to the next steps so they can get to their next meeting. These clients will likely be satisfied as long as you respond to their emails within four-to-six hours and deliver the results promised. They will probably never ask you about your family or vacation plans.

Other clients will be the exact opposite. For those who value relationships and connections, they may start every conversation by checking in on your personal life. In their case, prepare to extend the rapport building (you'll want to typically schedule longer meetings when you meet with these clients, so you're not rushed). Making sure they feel comfortable and showing you care about them and their objectives will be critical to a successful working relationship.

There will also be a subset of clients who don't engage in any rapport building with you because they don't see their relationship with you that way. There is no one-size-fits-all approach. What is perhaps most important to note is that your comfort level regarding rapport building is irrelevant—you need to flex to your clients, not the other way around. The more you match their preferred way of working and communicating, the more they'll appreciate their interactions with you.

One universal preference you can count on is that most people want to make the best use of their time. Always prepare before your meetings and keep the conversations focused on them. Before you speak with a company's CEO, listen to their company's latest earnings call. Don't ask your clients questions you can easily find answers to on your own. You can further extend the spotlight when you are attuned to your clients' job functions, professional ambitions, and personal goals. Figure out what they are concerned about and show that you've been paying attention. If you see something in the news that impacts your client, send them a quick note. If they are active on social media, take a look at what they've been posting. Keep the spotlight shining on them.

2. Step into Their Perspectives

When we assess an interaction, we normally focus on what we're getting out of it and whether it meets our expectations. However, research shows we build better connections with others when we see the world through their eyes.[5] We need to ask, "What are they hoping to achieve when they interact with us?" and "What are their expectations?"

Early in your business development career, you're likely to attend industry conferences and other events to broaden your network. Most professionals focused on business development prepare for those events by rehearsing their value proposition, reviewing the speaker and attendee lists, and double-checking that they have enough business cards to hand out. At these events, they focus on meeting as many people as possible, sharing their well-rehearsed elevator pitch whenever they sense an inkling of interest. What they often fail to consider is how the other person in the interaction sees them. If you approach each conversation with your agenda alone, you won't win any business or build any meaningful relationships. You might gather a stack of business cards, but business cards do not make a network (more on networking in Chapter 9).

If you've had a similar experience, consider a different approach. Instead of focusing on *your* goal to meet potential buyers, think about *their* motivation for attending conferences in the first place. They are often there for one of three main reasons: to learn best practices from other organizations; to connect with peers, trade notes, or find job opportunities; or to get away from the office and travel to an interesting city, all expenses paid. None of them are there to hear you pitch your services and help you build your book of business.

Recognizing these core motivations, and focusing on them, will increase your chances of connecting with your fellow attendees. If the conference is in your home city and you meet someone from out of town, suggest a local restaurant or must-see show. Instead of blurting out, "We do work with your company" to someone who works for an existing client, ask them what they think about the topics being discussed at the conference and how they plan to apply them at their firm. If you find two people who might benefit from meeting each other, try to connect them during the conference. This shift to focus more on others will lead to a much higher response rate in your post-conference follow-up. (Recommending a Broadway show with instructions on how to get half-priced tickets will make you more memorable than name-dropping your existing client list—trust me.)

Interacting with others in a way that shows you understand their perspective makes you more valuable to them in the moment. Of course, your job is not to be a conference concierge. Your job is to be helpful to others in the way *they* define "helpful." So, sometimes you might find yourself talking about what you do and in other situations you will avoid it entirely.

One caveat: To take someone else's perspective, we must make all sorts of assumptions, which creates an inherent danger. What if we assume wrong? Typically, we try to step into someone else's shoes by considering how they think and what they value.

However, if we try to take the perspective of someone whose life experience is different from ours, we may miss the mark. University of Chicago Professor Nicholas Epley's research[6] suggests that instead of *perspective-taking*, you should strive for *perspective-getting*. Instead of trying to read minds, ask questions and listen. Let the other person tell you what it's like to be them.

3. Show You Have Their Best Interests in Mind

When people feel like you are selling to them, they put up their defenses. But when you show them that you have their best interest in mind, you put them at ease and help them feel safe in collaborating with you. For some, giving them the chance to be heard and appearing genuinely interested in what they say may be enough. Others may need to see concrete actions as a signal that you care about them, and still others will only feel secure when they see results.

To keep people at ease, you'll want to understand what might trigger someone to react positively or negatively to you. According to neuroscience research, there are five dimensions that influence behavior in social interactions: status, certainty, autonomy, relatedness, and fairness (SCARF).[7] Like humans' survival instinct, each dimension responds to either rewards or threats. To help your clients feel positively about you, maximize rewards and minimize threats to each dimension.

For example, look for ways to enhance the other person's *status*—talk them up to their executives and avoid giving them unsolicited feedback. Give them *certainty* by outlining clear deliverables, sticking to agreed-upon timelines, and keeping them informed. Offer more *autonomy* by ceding control when possible and involving them in decisions. Foster *relatedness* by asking for input, connecting on a personal level, and staying non-judgmental of their ideas and perspective. Show *fairness* by being transparent and clarifying rules and terms. For your next client interaction, think of one SCARF dimension you can use to enhance your client's experience.

Another way to show you have your client's best interest in mind is to demonstrate that *you are a building block for their success* as opposed to them being a building block for yours. No one wants to be seen as a checkbook or the ticket to your next promotion. Remember, as harsh as this might sound, your clients do not care about you, your path to partnership, or your need to make a living. They care about how you can help them achieve their goals.

You sometimes need to subordinate your own needs for those of your client so they can see you're seriously thinking about them and invested in their success. Even a small gesture can go a long way. Mohamed Kande recommends taking a read of the environment to make sure you're focused on the clients' best interest in the moment. He recounts arriving for a meeting with a client and finding out they'd just come out of a four-hour operational review. Instead of going ahead with their scheduled meeting, Kande decided to chat with his client for a few minutes, then tell them, "I just wanted to say hello, and I'm happy to reschedule." In that way, he showed that he was attuned to his client needs in the moment. And though his client offered to keep the meeting, they ended up being thankful to get the unexpected time back. Even though Kande now had to reschedule it in his already busy week, he signaled that he was really looking out for the client. Kande shows, it's about prioritizing the long-term relationship rather than a specific meeting or transaction.

Kande's approach is just one specific example; there are many ways to make sure you are focusing on your clients' best interests:

- Give them your time and attention to fully understand their needs.

- Make yourself available.

- Recommend them to others who may be better at solving their problems than you.

- Be patient with their decision-making process, even though you might be behind on your revenue goals.

- Try to be flexible on pricing and payment terms if your client runs into a cash flow issue.

Even some basic language habits can help. Let's say that a client emails you about a new need that has arisen. They have a challenge and have thought of you as someone who might help. They view this challenge as a "need"; you consider it an "opportunity." If you state in your reply email, "I'm glad to discuss this new opportunity with you," you're focusing on yourself. This "need" may be distracting them from other tasks, and it is about to impact their budget. When you refer to it as an "opportunity," you're highlighting that this new "problem" for them is a "benefit" for you. That may undermine their trust. Instead, respond, "Sorry you're facing this challenge. We're glad to be a resource to help you address this."

One final point to keep in mind: Prioritizing your clients' interests does not mean blindly deferring to their point of view or suggestions. At times, you may need to tell your client something they don't want to hear and steer them toward a better solution. Creating tension with the client can be risky, but overall, the sycophant never becomes the trusted advisor. Your willingness to be a truth teller, even at the risk of losing your clients' business, shows you're focused on their needs. If you communicate your disagreement clearly and honestly, you show a genuine interest in doing right by your clients, and they will appreciate your candor and commitment to their success.

4. Avoid Being the Smartest Person in the Room

In addition to talking less about yourself, Mohamed Kande also recommends, "Never try to be the smartest person in the room." He recalls how so many professionals talk to show off what they know, rather than focus on giving their clients what they really need. If you are new to selling, this advice may sound counterintuitive. From your clients' viewpoint, wouldn't they want you to be "the smartest person in the room" if they are assessing whether to engage you to solve their problems? The short answer is "no." No matter how deep your expertise might be, you will not know more about your clients' business environment and issues than they do.

Let your client be the smartest person in the room (recall the "S" from SCARF—you want to increase their Status, not diminish it). If they produce the same idea you had, give them credit, and validate the idea by sharing where you've seen it work before. It could be easy for you to say that you also had the same idea, but remember, your client is not paying you to come up with solutions they can either come up with or execute on their own. Do what you can to protect your client. If, for example, your client misrepresents an inconsequential detail, decide if it's really necessary for you to correct them. There may be no win for you there. Again, your goal is to make them the smartest person in the room.

5. Make Giving Your Default

In his book *Give and Take*, Wharton Professor Adam Grant highlights three types of people: takers, matchers, and givers. Takers try to "serve themselves," matchers try to "get equal benefit for themselves and others," and givers try to "help others." Grant's research shows that giving is the best strategy because it works well regardless of the person you're engaging. Takers will feel like they are getting what they want from you. Matchers will owe you. Givers will recognize you as one of their own.

There are many ways to give. You can *give* your time, energy, money, connections, encouragement, or attention. If you think about these five behaviors to focus more on others, you're *giving* in one way or another—whether that's the spotlight, a sense of ease, a positive and client-focused interaction, or a deep respect for their experience.

According to Professor Grant, an effective giver does the following:

- Goes out of their way to help people they meet
- Gives with no strings attached; doesn't keep score or look for quid pro quo
- Gives something that *truly* helps the other person

In business development, you can show that you're a giver by offering value in every interaction, not just a promise of value. Often, sales conversations promise value once the client buys, such as "You can get all of these benefits if you just hire me." At best, this is a Matcher's strategy. At worst, it's a Taker's strategy. To be a Giver, identify something of value you can give your prospects—without expecting anything in return. For example, you can share useful industry information, make an introduction to other people who can help your client, or create an opportunity to enhance your client's visibility. Always think about how you can make it worthwhile for them to spend time with you. Whether it is an introduction, a relevant insight, or an iced coffee, don't show up empty-handed.

That all said, keep the following in mind: A surprising result in Grant's research is that givers are both the best *and* worst performers. Grant notes that *successful* givers tend to give "five-minute favors," opportunities to offer high value to others at a minimal cost to the giver. Givers who were too altruistic ended up with the lowest productivity and results. You must be smart about your giving, thoughtfully selecting when, where, how, and to whom you give. You don't want to burn out by giving at the expense of your own well-being. When it comes down to it, your ability to focus on others has limits.

Can You Focus Too Much on Others?

Sometimes a lack of business development success may stem from too little self-orientation rather than too much. If you give away too much of your time or too many of your services for free, you'll have a challenging time gaining traction for your own sales momentum. You don't need to sacrifice your needs to become less self-oriented. If you find that you sacrifice your own needs more than you should, try to think about the people who may rely on *your* success: your family who needs you to pay the mortgage, your employees who depend on you for their salaries, or your clients who need you to keep investing in your learning so you can better serve them.

The goal is to stay attuned to your clients' needs without ignoring your own. Success in sales requires a balance of empathy and ego drive—empathy to be attuned to your client's issues; ego drive to persist until you seal the deal.[8] Helping your clients buy is securing permission from them to solve their problems for fair compensation. Through consistent focus on the client, you'll build the trust needed to be seen as their assistant buyer.

Self-Reflection Questions

1. How can I be an assistant buyer to my client?

2. Whom do I trust deeply? What attributes make them trustworthy?

3. Would I consider myself high in warmth and competence? What can I do to enhance both dimensions further?

4. What is one concrete way I can deepen trust with an existing or potential client by increasing my warmth, competence, or both?

5. What can I do differently to focus more on my clients? Of the five behaviors, which one do I need to work on the most to shift to a client-focused mindset?

6. What's one thing I can do to appeal to my client's sense of status, certainty, autonomy, relatedness, and fairness?

7. Can I identify takers, matchers, and givers?

8. How effective am I when advocating for my own needs?

CHAPTER

4

Realistically Optimistic

Chapter 4: Realistically Optimistic

As a rainmaker, you will get rejected.

Whether that rejection comes in the form of someone choosing your competitor, not responding to your outreach, or asking you to take them off your mailing list, you will hear more "no's" than "yeses." And the rejections won't stop, no matter how seasoned you become or how big your book of business. The difference between those who become rainmakers and those who don't, though, is the fortitude to keep swimming through the sea of rejections. People with staying power keep striving toward success because they remain hopeful, or said in another way, they are optimistic. Optimism gets us out of bed and helps us endure the grind. When we're knocked down, optimism forces us back up. And in the end, we're rewarded for our efforts. As Nat Friedman, CEO of the multi-billion-dollar IT services company GitHub, says, "Pessimists sound smart. Optimists make money."[1]

Now, optimism alone is not enough. In *Succeed: How We Can Reach Our Goals*, motivation researcher Heidi Grant Halvorson states, "Thinking positively about your chances of success is important but believing you'll easily succeed is dangerous and not helpful."[2] To help you succeed, you'll want to give yourself positive reasons for why success is possible, while also planning ahead for the inevitable obstacles to come (and in sales, there will be no shortage of them).[3] *Realistic* optimism comes from maintaining hope that you will succeed while simultaneously facing reality, seeking to understand and address why you haven't yet succeeded. Sometimes, you didn't close the deal because the client decided to hit pause on the initiative. Other times, it's because you were not effective in your interactions with the client. *Unrealistic* optimism is the belief that everything will work out just fine without any adjustment on your part. People with this type of optimism are bound to be disappointed.

Rainmakers do not blindly expect every pitch to result in business, or every client to stay with them forever, but they do think positively and remain optimistic, especially when they experience rejection or other setbacks. Their resilience helps them bounce back, adapt, and persevere when they're not seeing results. It's easy to focus on the negatives when things don't go our way, allowing our pessimism to get the best of us. Realistically, to stay optimistic, we must understand how optimism works while maintaining a true sense of our business development abilities. If we give up whenever we meet some resistance or don't see immediate success, we'll have a hard time developing a healthy book of business.

Get through the Dip with Grit

Author Seth Godin argues that "almost everything in life worth doing is controlled by the Dip."[4] He describes the Dip as "the long stretch between beginner's luck and real accomplishment" or "the seventh time you fall on your butt while learning to snowboard." It is often difficult to see the long-term promised land when you're struggling in the short-term. *Grit*, a term encompassing hard work and perseverance over time, is what gets you through the Dip. Grit bridges your short-term efforts with your long-term payoff by giving you the patient persistence to connect these time horizons. Most of you achieved your current level of expertise and success through grit, and the same will hold true as you build your book of business.

One of the foremost researchers on the relationship between grit and achievement is University of Pennsylvania Professor Angela Duckworth. Whether it's West Point military cadets, or new teachers at challenging schools, Duckworth found that an individual's grit is a better predictor of long-term success than that individual's talent or IQ.[5] In her book, *Grit: The Power of Passion and Perseverance*, she defines grit as the "disposition to pursue long-term goals with both passion and perseverance." She breaks the idea down using a two-part equation:

1. Talent × Effort = Skill
2. Skill × Effort = Achievement

Duckworth explains, "Talent is how quickly your skills improve when you invest effort. Achievement is what happens when you take your acquired skills and use them." Effort is the key driver in both instances and unlocks the potential of your talent and skill. There are no shortcuts to long-term business development success. Don't waste time looking for sales secrets or hacks—you have to put in the work.

It is painful to fail in any endeavor, but heartbreaking when you feel you've given it your all. It's during these times when you most need grit to help you persist. And, as long as you stay the course, working diligently despite setbacks, failure will lead to growth. Grit should therefore be thought of in terms of stamina. In business development, this stamina pays off in three ways. First, you will find it easier to add value to others as you deepen your skills, knowledge, and relationships. Second, the harder you work, the more you'll value what you accomplish and the more difficult it will be for others to replicate. Last, performing well because you've put in the effort will motivate you and cause you to enjoy your work more.[6]

To develop grit, in addition to plugging into your interests (covered in Chapter 2) and focusing on the purposeful work to improve your clients' lives (discussed in Chapter 3), Professor Duckworth suggests being hopeful about the future—it is easier to press on when you trust things will get better. Believing in your ability to overcome obstacles goes a long way. In fact, the more optimistic you are about your eventual success, the more grit you'll show. And even if you're more of a glass-half-empty kind of person by nature, optimism can be learned and cultivated.

Learned Optimism

When something good or bad happens to us, we ask ourselves, "Why?" According to research by University of Pennsylvania Professor Martin Seligman, how we answer that question will determine whether we look at a situation optimistically or pessimistically.[7] To be more optimistic, when something bad happens, explain the cause as external, temporary, and specific, as opposed to personal, permanent, and pervasive. For example, if one of your current clients leaves you for a competitor, avoid explanations like, "I am terrible at this. I should have seen this coming. Our service is becoming less and less competitive (personal). My other clients are likely going to leave (pervasive). I'm never going to succeed in sales (permanent)."

Instead, adopt a more optimistic and productive explanation:

> It's unfortunate they decided to go this route, but they are a tough client and some days you win and some days you lose (external). Hopefully, when comparing our service to our competitors, they'll realize that they received above-and-beyond treatment, and reconsider us next year (temporary). Let me stay in touch and continue to offer value. I'm glad it was limited just to this client and my other clients are happy with us (specific).

Next time something bad happens, pay attention to how you explain the cause. If you're curious about your default explanatory style, take a Learned Optimism test. (You can find one online with a quick search for "learned optimism test.")

When you are optimistic, your attention gravitates toward the good things that are happening with your business development efforts. When a client declines to meet with you, instead of focusing on the rejection, you focus on the fact that this person responded to you in the first place. Optimism also positively impacts your mental and physical well-being.[8] It will help you deal with the stress that comes with carrying a revenue quota. You'll take fewer sick days. You'll bounce back faster when you don't hit your goals. Optimism will also help you attract clients and collaborators—no one wants to work with a Debbie or Drew Downer.

Another way to stay optimistic is to recognize what you can control and accept what you cannot. Imagine you're driving on the highway on your way home from work. Just before you hit your exit ramp, a car suddenly cuts you off, causing you to swerve and almost hit the guardrail. How would you feel? How would you respond? When I run this thought experiment in my workshops, most people say they would feel angry after their initial fear or surprise, then respond with—you guessed it—cursing. In this situation, you had a stimulus (person cutting you off), you felt an emotion (getting angry), and you had a reaction (cursing). You can't control being cut off, but you can control how you respond. The key is to recognize that there is a step in-between the stimulus and reaction that determines your emotion: your interpretation of the stimulus. If you reacted angrily, you likely believed the person who cut you off was irresponsible and reckless. But if you found out the person who cut you off was rushing to the hospital because of a sudden emergency, your anger would quickly subside.

When our emotions hijack us, they may lead us to act in ways counter to our own interests. If we're overcome by road rage, we may drive recklessly, which takes away from our goal to safely get home. In most situations, we will never know the true intention of the other person's actions. The good news about not knowing the truth is we can *choose* the interpretation that will help us respond in a way that aligns with our goals. For example, consider cold calling. Cold calls can be emotionally trying because you'll likely get no response or a rejection. When a prospect does not respond to you or is uninterested in learning about your services (the stimulus), you might personalize their response, thinking you are bothering them or that your offerings are subpar (your interpretation). This thought may lead you to feeling discouraged (the emotion), which will give you pause to reach out to other potential clients (your response).

Instead, choose an interpretation that will help you stay optimistic and continue your outreach. Perhaps your prospect wants to hear from you, but they are busy due to an internal crisis. With this interpretation, you see their response as a "not now," as opposed to a "no," which will help you to keep following up. You can reframe your interpretation anytime you find yourself in a negative state. What's empowering about choosing your interpretation is that it changes not only your emotion and response, but the response of the other person as well. Your response becomes the stimulus that other people will interpret to influence how they react to you, as highlighted in Figure 4.1.

Reflect on a recent challenging interaction you had with a client. Now ask yourself the following questions in sequence (sample responses have been provided for guidance):

Q: What negative emotion did I experience?

A: Anger.

Q: What specific behavior triggered that emotion?

A: The client criticized our proposal.

Q: What was my interpretation of my client's behavior?

A: They don't think we're sophisticated or good enough.

Q: What was my initial reaction?

A: I disengaged from the conversation and took on a "take it or leave it" attitude since the client seemed impossible to please.

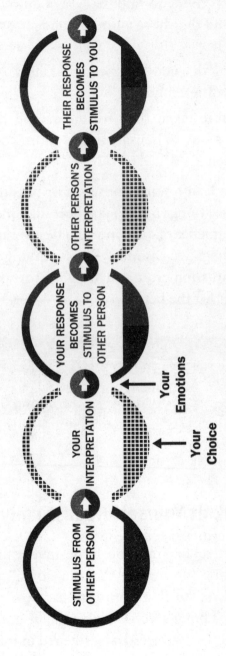

FIGURE 4.1 Choosing Your Response to Influence Their Response

The following labels appear within the figure:

STIMULUS FROM OTHER PERSON

YOUR INTERPRETATION

Your Choice

Your Emotions

YOUR RESPONSE BECOMES STIMULUS TO OTHER PERSON

OTHER PERSON'S INTERPRETATION

THEIR RESPONSE BECOMES STIMULUS TO YOU

Q: How could I have interpreted my situation differently?

A: The client is trying to find the best solution to solve their problem, and they have a limited budget, so they need to get this right.

Q: Considering this new interpretation, how would I have responded differently?

A: I should have taken time to understand their feedback and found a way to help them feel more confident about the approach.

Whether you lean toward optimism or pessimism, you can shift the way you see things to help you become a more successful rainmaker. This sequence of questions can be leveraged whenever you experience a negative emotion. By identifying what you can control in that situation, you will be able to take purposeful action to change it for the better.

Practical Tip

For a quick boost of positivity, write down one thing you're grateful for in the last 24 hours along with a specific reason why.

Look at Yourself Realistically

Before we all start scheduling hourly positive affirmations and giving ourselves one too many "You can do it!" pep talks, it's important to understand that optimism can work against us if we're not careful. Though we want to remain optimistic about our outlook for success, we need to be steeped in reality, honestly assessing our abilities, opportunities, and goals. Positivity can go wrong when we distort reality or otherwise lie to ourselves. As American physicist Richard Feynman reminds us, "The first principle is that you must not fool yourself—and you are the easiest person to fool."[9]

According to billionaire hedge fund manager Ray Dalio, "An accurate understanding of reality is the essential foundation for any good outcome."[10] In business development, that means working with the reality of business development as it is, and not as we wish it would be. In rainmaking, your revenue number is reality, so you must own that number. Whenever you don't hit your revenue target, reflect on this question: "What might I be missing that has led to this result?" For example, you might have missed your goal because one of your large clients left you, and you didn't have enough opportunities in your pipeline to fill the gap. This experience will help you update your reality to account for unexpected client attrition going forward.

You also need to own the fact that sometimes, when you lose a deal, it's because you're just not skilled enough at selling, at least not yet. In that situation, it is important to ask, "What abilities need to be further developed for me to reach my goal?" For example, if you didn't make your goal this year because you were swamped with billable work and didn't have time for outreach, you likely need to improve your ability to balance client delivery and business development. Or you need to build the right-size team so you can delegate work more effectively (as shown further in Chapter 12). An optimistic outlook will give you the courage to honestly confront your shortcomings and assess your weaknesses, the mistakes you've made, and the types of challenges that stood in the way of reaching your goals. Often, those obstacles continue to block us because we don't admit our mistakes or shore up our weaknesses. By strengthening your grip on reality whenever you experience the pain of losing a deal or missing your goal, you increase your chances of achieving your goal the next time around.

Bounce Back and Get Your Head in the Game

As a rainmaker your optimism will be put to the test. Whenever you experience a setback, you may get stuck in a way of thinking that distorts reality,[11] making it harder to bounce back. A practical way to catch yourself from falling into these mind traps is to be attuned to your emotions and self-talk. Whenever you don't achieve the outcome you wanted or expected, try to recognize how you're feeling and what you're saying to yourself. Negative statements like "I should have leveraged my network more," "My firm is not supporting me enough," "I'm going to be deferred again for my promotion," or "Why even try if it's not going to make a difference?" all indicate you may be caught in a mind trap.

These statements are likely accompanied by frustration, guilt, anger, hopelessness, and other emotions that keep you ruminating on the same negative thoughts. Whenever you're in this situation, and especially when you feel like giving up, your goal is to break out of this cycle of negative thinking and return to a place of emotional positivity, or at least neutrality. Once your head is back in the game, you can productively respond to the setback by seeing reality more accurately. To escape these mind traps, leverage the following "real-time resilience" skills[12]:

- **Use vivid evidence.** Whenever you find yourself focusing on negative emotions, challenge them by using the phrase, "That's not true because . . . (vivid evidence)." For example, if you feel anxious because you think your firm will let you go if you don't recover from missing your quarterly target, you can disrupt this mind trap by saying, "That's not true because 100 percent of my colleagues who missed their quarterly revenue targets were not let go."

- **Reframe the situation.** Changing the interpretation of a stimulus, as discussed earlier in the chapter, will help you reframe by changing the way you feel about the stimulus. When you find yourself stuck in a negative thought cycle, reframe in real-time using the phrase, "A more helpful way to see this is. . ." If you feel angry because your client is dismissing you and your firm, tell yourself, "A more helpful way to see this is that the client is going to help me become better, which will only help to grow my book of business."

- **Have a contingency plan.** A good way to prevent paralysis in the face of a setback is to be realistic about the outcome and have a plan ready in response. Instead of focusing on the best-case or worst-case outcomes, consider what is most likely going to happen. Then build a contingency plan for the likely outcome. To use this skill in real-time, whenever you're catastrophizing, say, "A more likely outcome is X, and if that happens, I will Y to deal with it." As you're going into the final pitch to a potential client, you might set a rule, "A more likely outcome is the client choosing to stay with the incumbent, and if that happens, I will grab a drink with my colleagues to thank them. I'll then chalk it up to 'you win some and you lose some,' and get back to my client follow-up list."

Other ways to reset from negative thinking is to find humor, when possible, stay away from negative input, and get some sleep. Most of our jobs don't deal with life-and-death situations, so when we find ourselves becoming overly serious, there might be an opportunity for levity. We can also be knocked back into negative thinking when the information or people around us trigger that response. To avoid this situation, limit the negative news you consume and spend time with other optimists. Lastly, we fall into mind traps more easily when we are tired or depleted. One of the best ways to recharge is to get ample rest.

Better Than Before

Resilience is not just about bouncing back; it's about bouncing back and *being better than before* the setback. Once you're in a positive emotional state, you'll be able to recognize rejection for what it truly is: a data point to help you improve your sales process and activities. If your prospect didn't choose you, it could be for a number of reasons. Maybe they didn't believe in your approach; received pressure to go with their boss's old classmate; or ran out of time to onboard a new external resource.

By staying optimistic about your success and realistic about your abilities, you now have a learning opportunity before you. Ask yourself what you could have done differently to land the business. If the prospect didn't believe in your approach, you might work on the way you diagnose the problem or present your solution. If they went with their boss's old classmate, think of how you might be able to find out who else is in the running in the future to avoid any extra work on your end (old classmates or roommates are hard to beat). Better yet, develop your own executive relationships. If they ran out of time, you might look at how you can drive the process forward more quickly next time.

The reason prospects decide not to do business with us is rarely personal. In fact, people think about us a lot less than we think. When someone rejects us, we may feel that they won't just remember us, they'll be annoyed by us if we reach out to them again in the future. This fear causes us to stop our pursuit, removing the possibility of ever working with this individual. But think of the last person who reached out to you cold, and you didn't need what they wanted to sell you. You probably gave them very little thought—if any at all. I would be shocked if you remembered any of their names.

In reality, when you reach out to someone and don't have a good conversation, if they either ignored you or dismissed you, then they won't remember you, the company you work for, and certainly not your name. People have short-lived memories when it comes to interactions that don't amount to much. Unless you've really made an effort to annoy or anger someone, most will not expend the mental energy to remember you. More likely, you just weren't important or relevant to them at that time. And that's a plus, because that means you get to try again to either make a better impression the next time around or catch them when they have a real need and would be open to speaking with you. Not giving up allows you to keep refining your approach as you move forward toward rainmaking success.

Bet on Yourself

By improving your game each time you bounce back from a setback, you should feel more confident about betting on yourself to succeed. If you're lucky to have a great manager, robust network, or abundant firm support, you should feel even better about your chances. If you have none of these, you should still feel optimistic—researchers have found that scarcity, combined with necessity, forces people to be more creative with their resources.[13] Instead of *lamenting* your constraints, redirect your energy to *working with* your constraints. Be curious about why something worked or didn't work for you. If people don't reply to you, recognize what you need to do to change their experience and get their response. Don't just hope it will work out— take charge.

Generating sustainable revenue and building a strong network and reputation takes time. By stepping into the mindset of being realistically optimistic, you'll find that when you bet on yourself, and you keep going, your success will become inevitable.

Self-Reflection Questions

1. How have I demonstrated grit in my previous achievements? What gave me staying power?

2. What is one thing I can do today to be more optimistic?

3. Thinking back to a time when I felt a negative emotion, what was my interpretation of the stimulus in that situation? How might I reframe it and what would I do differently?

4. Do I look at rejection as feedback and an opportunity for growth or as a limiting factor to building my book of business?

5. Am I willing to bet on myself?

Confidently Humble

Chapter 5: Confidently Humble

While going through a few old boxes that had been tucked away in the garage, I found some of my books from when I was in junior high. Among them were a handful of Greek myths and tragedies. As I thumbed through the pages, I was reminded of how surprised I was as a kid at how so many of these stories were about hubris being a fatal flaw. Whether Oedipus, Icarus, or Tantalus, excessive pride *always* came before their fall (for Icarus, it was a literal fall). Like many adolescents, I filed this lesson into my good-to-know-but-it'll-never-happen-to-me folder. I didn't see myself as a proud person, and I couldn't fathom how anyone could let their sense of pride ever get so far away from them that it would harm them or, worse yet, cause their downfall. Well, like any other kid, I had a lot to learn.

Early in my tenure at Exec|Comm, I found out the hard way that hubris can sometimes just sneak up on us. I had been working with a client whose executives had given me some excellent reviews, and I had built up a strong rapport with their head of talent development. I thought I was "in." One day, I had a call with the client and a new team member. My buyer had just agreed to the approach we'd laid out, when he introduced me to his new hire. After some quick pleasantries, the newbie asked me, "Could you send me an updated proposal detailing how you might address functional and regional differences, language capabilities, inconsistent access to technology. . .?" And the list dragged on.

Sure, sure, I thought, as I muted my phone and breathed a sigh of annoyance, no problem, I'll just repurpose something I already had sitting around and send it along. As mentioned, I was sure I was in the company's good graces, the boss seemed to already agree to the project, and sending a proposal felt like nothing more than a formality. Why waste any time jumping through unnecessary hoops? How much weight would the new hire's request really carry? So, I hit copy, paste, send, and didn't give it another thought.

After two weeks, I still hadn't heard back from the client, so I touched base with them. "Hi," I wrote in my email, "just following up on the proposal I sent over. Wanted to see if you're ready to pin down timing." The new team member replied later that day. "Sorry," they said, "we decided to choose another resource that had a better fit for our specific needs. We'll keep you in mind for future opportunities."

Maybe you're saying, "Robert, what were you thinking?" Or "I would *never* do that." And honestly, I never thought I would either—until I did. Instead of giving this person the time and attention they required, I brushed them off. At the time, I was coming off a few big wins with this client. When this opportunity came up, I felt I already earned these new engagements because of the work I'd already done. When I was introduced to my contact's new team member, I thought this person would follow my lead since I was more knowledgeable about the company and had more history working with them. I figured they would just be the order-taker. If anything went wrong, I could always go to their boss. But in the end, my generic proposal wasn't what they were looking for, and once their decision was made, it was final.

Simply said, I forgot my place. I was arrogant and completely misguided to think the way I did. I had an inaccurate view of where I stood with the client, and I didn't appreciate my new contact's contributions to the process. They were looking to add value in their new role, and I mistakenly assumed they were there to check the boxes. My overconfidence and lack of humility—the belief that *I knew better* in this situation—single-handedly derailed a multi-year deal. I'll never forget the lesson I learned: *Success tends to inflate our self-importance; bad things happen when our self-importance over-inflates.*

When we begin seeing success as rainmakers, it becomes easier and easier to fall into these traps. We tend not to think of ourselves as having inflated egos, and we're unlikely to notice this transformation taking place. Unfortunately, if we're not thinking about it, it's not a matter of *if* this will happen, it's a matter of *when* it will happen—even the most successful rainmakers need to keep themselves in check. The best way to prevent our ego from derailing us is to cultivate humility and not take our clients, or anyone for that matter, for granted. Still, we must be confident enough to recognize our strengths and the value we bring to our clients. In this way, we need to balance between humility, or being humble, and confidence.

In *Think Again: The Power of Knowing What You Don't Know*, Professor Adam Grant defines *confident humility* as "having faith in our capability while appreciating that we may not have the right solution or even be addressing the right problem."[1] This way of thinking allows us to see the nuances of a situation and apply our expertise more effectively. Research shows that humility also helps us be more flexible and adaptable to our surroundings.[2] Confident humility encourages us to be curious about other solutions, an exploration that will help us better serve our clients. We need to believe in ourselves while still questioning our approach, our perspective, and, maybe most importantly, our self-importance.

Your Ego Is Your Enemy

If you ask ten people how they would define humility, you will likely get ten different definitions. Some people equate being humble with being meek or modest. Others describe it as self-sacrifice. One practical definition comes from researchers who analyzed different descriptions of humility in organizations and converged on three core elements:[3]

- Willingness to view oneself accurately
- Appreciation of others' strengths and contributions
- Teachability and openness to new ideas and feedback

Humility is a quality based on the perception of others, which can make it challenging to develop. According to researchers Bradley P. Owens, Michael D. Johnson, and Terence R. Mitchell, humility is "usually a label attached by others—not something an individual assesses and asserts as part of his or her own self-view."[4] We can't deem ourselves humble; we need to be *given* that label.

Ego—described by author Ryan Holiday as an "unhealthy belief in our own importance"[5]—gets in the way of our humility. In his book, *Ego Is the Enemy*, Holiday asserts that our ego undermines us when we're striving for our goals, derails us when we're successful, and keeps us down when we fail. When you first shift from doing the work to selling the work, you'll likely be diligent and conscientious. You'll work with senior rainmakers to create a business development plan, network with centers of influence, and hone your selling skills. As you consistently work your plan, you will begin to see your efforts pay off. Your clients will consider you for more opportunities. You will advance to more final rounds. Eventually, you will begin landing deals and winning business—maybe you already are.

As you deliver more successful engagements, people around you will begin recognizing your contributions. Your peers or more junior team members will ask you for advice. Your leaders may even label you a superstar, put you on partner track, and give you access to key accounts. Your clients might ask to deal with you exclusively, while members of your network reach out to collaborate.

Sounds great, right? But all of these accolades will slowly inflate your ego, and you won't even realize it. If we leave our egos unchecked, we start believing in our own hype, thinking our clients are lucky to work with us or our firm is fortunate to have us, and not the other way around. We assume our way of doing things is better than everyone else's. We may even feel we've "figured out" this whole rainmaking business and find ourselves judging others who are not as successful as we are.

When ego takes over, we can end up falling into two counter-productive mindsets that undermine the rainmaker mindset: complacency and self-centeredness. If we think we've "made it," we're likely to become complacent. Our complacency causes us to spend less time preparing for meetings and engagements, reduces our proactive outreach to prospects, and leads us to *stop* developing ourselves as rainmakers. All the activities that helped us become a rainmaker may seem less important or less urgent since we now "know what we're doing."

When we become self-centered, we fixate on ourselves, putting energy into being "justly rewarded": the fair compensation, the right title, the proper recognition. In doing so, we re-channel our energy to be recognized for our contributions, diverting attention away from work that adds value to our clients—work that got us to this point in the first place. We confuse impressing people with being truly impressive.[6] Our ego fools us into making recognition our goal, and we forget that acknowledgment comes as a by-product of our real accomplishments.

Ego takes us away from long-term rainmaking success, but we're often unaware when our egos begin growing. To help raise self-awareness of an inflating ego, and how to quickly keep it in check, look out for the warning signs in Table 5.1 and test out the suggested responses.

Table 5.1   Ego Inflation Warning Signs and Remedies

Warning Signs	Remedies
You believe you are special and the best at what you do.	Maybe you're currently the best at what you do around *your* office, but there's always someone out there who is better (if not today, then tomorrow).
You're certain your way is better; you're unable or unwilling to meet others on their terms.	Your way is one way, not the best way. Remind yourself, if there is anything to be certain about, it's that you're likely missing something in your approach.
You feel entitled to other people's attention, time, or business.	Think of a situation when someone acted entitled to your attention, time, or business—how annoying was that?
You feel you deserve to succeed and are destined for great things.	Who says? For a quick fix, just swap the grandiose "deserve to" and "destined for" with "can" and "can do."
You feel slighted when you don't get what you want, and you believe those around you are not deserving of their success.	No one made you the judge of success, and no one cares that you feel slighted. Get over yourself.
You spend more time talking about what you've done instead of accomplishing new goals.	Get back to work!
You give unsolicited advice, interrupt others when speaking, and forcefully assert your opinions on all matters despite your level of expertise.	In the words of Aaron Burr, as depicted in *Hamilton: An American Musical*, "Talk less. Smile more."

If you recognize any of these thoughts or behaviors in yourself, your ego might be getting the best of you. Review your business development activities over the last three, six, and twelve months. If you see your client outreach dwindling, your ego might be fooling you into believing your clients will now come to you, and you no longer need to prospect. You can also assess your weekly activities, noting whether you're focused on serving others or serving yourself. For example, are you spending time internally promoting your accomplishments or complaining about being underappreciated rather than creating new ways to support your clients or reaching out to more prospects? Be attuned to any impulses to seek recognition or validation for what you're doing, and don't confuse recognition as a proxy for real accomplishment.

Once you see your ego as your enemy, you'll be able to better guard against it. But don't confuse keeping your ego in check with projecting less confidence. Some people struggle with humility because they fear losing their edge. Others may resist it because they fear appearing timid. These beliefs stem from mistakenly linking confidence with ego. In reality, you can be confident without being egotistical—they are not one and the same.

Practical Tip

In ancient Rome when triumphant generals were celebrated for a day and promoted, "however temporarily—above every mortal Roman," they would have a companion standing next to them reminding them of their own mortality (*memento mori*) to help the generals keep their egos in check.[7] Remember *memento mori*—the next time you receive praise, remind yourself that it's just a temporary acknowledgment of your success, which will need to be earned again and again.

Confidence versus Ego

As advisors to your clients, you need to show and instill confidence. Your confidence stems from the hard work you've put in to build your expertise. Being humble does not mean downplaying your knowledge and expertise. Humility is a result of being open to the idea that other people may know something you don't. You can be certain that your clients and prospects will know better than you regarding their situation and what they want from you. When you interact with your clients, you don't need to agree with their perspective, but you do need to understand where they're coming from so you can help them. Humility creates space for that understanding. Meanwhile, confidence provides you with the belief that you can, indeed, help your clients solve their problems and reach their goals.

In an ideal world, our confidence should match our competence. Unfortunately, this rarely happens. Early in our career, or when we take on a new role, our self-confidence is typically low because we recognize our *incompetence*. As we work hard to fill our skill gap, our competence begins to outpace our confidence. We'll likely start experiencing impostor syndrome, as our senior colleagues place us in situations where they have more confidence in us than we have in ourselves. Luckily, research shows that impostor syndrome may not be a bad thing: People who feel this way are highly motivated to work hard to stop feeling like an impostor.[8] When we make it through challenging situations unscathed, our confidence increases.

Early in my career, my firm's former Managing Partner, Lisa Bennis, would tell me, "You're an expert way before *you'll believe* you are." At first, I didn't buy it. I felt as if I was bumbling my way through my work, just as I had ruined the deal mentioned at the start of this chapter. In my client interactions, I would try to showcase my knowledge, highlight my skills, and play up my career accomplishments. When we're unproven, we focus on trying to prove ourselves, and there is nothing wrong with that when we need to establish our credibility. Bennis validates this point, "Up until this part of your career, you have been rewarded for building and communicating your expertise." But that all changes. In business development, your credibility is expected; that's why your prospect is willing to meet with you in the first place. You no longer need to prove your worth. You must shift from explaining who you are to showing your clients how you can serve them.

Bennis recalls that it took her quite some time to make this mindset shift, but she eventually got there. "I finally stopped trying to prove my expertise and chose to shift the whole paradigm," she explains. "I will make this meeting about learning from the other person, and I'm not going to worry one bit about demonstrating how smart I am . . ." Not only was she confident in herself, but she also removed any potential complications that could have arisen if she came in thinking she "knew best." Instead of leading with her ego, she led with both confidence and humility. "Every time I approached the client meeting focused on learning, I've had success, with success being defined as furthering the relationship or winning an engagement. Now, it's at the heart of how I approach every client conversation."

As we become more seasoned and our competence is recognized more widely, we run the risk of our confidence not only catching up with our competence but potentially racing far ahead. When we are more confident than we are competent, our ego overinflates. This overconfidence causes us to stop learning, which further widens the gap between our confidence and competence. Our ego begins whispering to us, "You can do no wrong," or "You're invaluable," and we begin to act in ways to protect our self-worth rather than become more valuable to our clients. We start to dismiss constructive feedback, put down other people's accomplishments, and refuse to consider colleagues' ideas. In short, like a weed, if unchecked, our ego can grow to choke out our humility. But by actively cultivating our humility—and pulling the weeds of ego right when they appear—we can tap into the benefits of being confidently humble.

Cultivate Humility

According to research, humble people focus "on their inter-dependence with others rather than their independence from others."[9] To cultivate humility and foster interdependence, we must strive to be more objective about our abilities and limitations, more appreciative of others' strengths and contributions, and more open to feedback, ideas, and the opinion of others. These three elements are intertwined. We're more objective about our abilities when we're more open to others' perspective. We're more open to others' feedback and ideas when we appreciate their strengths and contributions. We are more appreciative of others' strengths when we are objective about our own abilities.

Let's take a look at each element in turn. At the end of each section, three statements are shown to help you assess and consider how humble you come across to others (these are based on the Expressed Humility Scale, developed by Owens, Johnson, and Mitchell[10]). The more strongly you agree with each statement, the more likely others perceive you as being humble. Ideally, you'll want others to assess you on these statements. No matter your starting point, you can still cultivate humility through the suggestions provided.

Be More Objective in Your Self-Evaluation

It's difficult to accurately assess how we contribute to our wins and losses. When we look back at our historical revenue numbers, we'll likely remember the hard work we put in, and the clear strategy we pursued, but remain oblivious to the luck and other invisible factors that may have impacted our success. We're rarely objective in assessing our abilities and contributions. When I reflect on my early successes, there's a strong chance my clients engaged me because of my firm's reputation, the reputation of one of my partners, or the significant guidance and support I received from my senior colleagues. It doesn't help that the longer I am at the firm, the more credit is misattributed to me for those early successes. I have caught myself mistakenly thinking I succeeded because *I* made things happen.

Since we often skew toward being overly positive about our abilities, we can counterbalance this tendency by not only acknowledging the role of luck and the contribution of others' in our wins, but also reminding ourselves of our limitations. Focusing on our limitations requires us to be vulnerable. We display vulnerability when we try new approaches, step out of our comfort zone, and seek out difficult challenges. Typically, these experiences are humbling because we don't know what we're doing—and we're likely not doing it well. We're typically falling flat on our faces with not much to show for it.

Social scientist Brené Brown points out that people often see vulnerability as "courage in you and weakness in me," emphasizing how vulnerability is humanizing.[11] It's not easy to show vulnerability, but if we can do it in a sincere way, it will keep our ego in check and help us connect more deeply with others. Instead of always putting our best foot forward, we might try sharing a struggle or letting people in on our disappointments. (A quick word to the wise: Do this only if others already see you as highly competent;[12] if you haven't proven yourself yet, highlighting your flaws can make you seem less competent.) Further, try getting comfortable with saying, "I don't know." Although you will be the expert, you don't know everything. When you admit you don't know something, you show confidence in your own standing while being vulnerable. Similarly, you also display confident humility when you turn down work that is outside your circle of competence. Although you'll be able to solve many of your clients' issues, you won't be able to solve all of them.

Expressed Humility Statements
- I actively seek feedback, even if it's critical.
- I admit it when I don't know how to do something.
- I acknowledge when others have more knowledge and skills than I do.

Be More Appreciative of Others' Strengths and Contributions

In a survey of Stanford MBA students, 87 percent rated their academic performance as above the median.[13] In a study of driving competency, 93 percent of American drivers believe their driving ability is above average.[14] In an impromptu debate with my spouse, I thought I was more than pulling my weight with chores at home (she quickly disproved this). We often overestimate our contribution and underestimate others' contributions because we see 100 percent of what we do and only a tiny percentage of what others do. Part of cultivating humility is to be aware of this dynamic and actively increase our valuation of other people, without decreasing our self-valuation.[15]

When ego takes over, and we're looking for our own recognition, we forget that other people welcome attention and credit just like we do. To help you be more appreciative, look for ways to champion others' strengths. Executive coach Randall Stutman advocates being a *fan* of those around you. How can you show people you're truly rooting for them, whether they're having a good day or an off day? Instead of focusing on what your colleagues can do better, genuinely highlight their strengths and acknowledge their contributions. Think of a recent client win and send your colleague a note citing a specific way they've helped make that win happen.

The more you give credit to others, the more likely they will support your success, because when you win, they win. Focusing on how others contribute does not take away from what you contribute. When you're closing deals, assess how others might have helped you succeed and recognize their work. Whenever possible, talk up a colleague to one of your executives or clients. True humility is finding ways to lift up others without putting ourselves down.[16]

Expressed Humility Statements

- I take notice of others' strengths.
- I often compliment others on their strengths.
- I show appreciation for the unique contribution of others.

Be More Open to Feedback, Ideas, and Opinions

Research shows our brains give more weight to information that confirms our beliefs, while discounting information that disconfirms them (also known as confirmation bias).[17] In many instances, we don't even seek out a contrary opinion. Professor Grant, whom we mentioned earlier, laments that "when it comes to our own knowledge and opinions, we often favor feeling right over being right."[18] He highlights three personas we may slip into when we interact with others: preachers, prosecutors, and politicians. We become preachers when we think we're right; prosecutors when we believe others are wrong; and politicians when we seek the approval or support of others.[19] Any time we fall into one of these roles, it becomes harder for us to challenge our own views.

To be open to others' thoughts and ideas, Grant suggests taking on the role of a scientist. Scientists stay openminded because they focus on what they *don't* know, actively searching for ways they might be wrong. As you probably remember from grade school, experiments start with a hypothesis or educated guess, and the goal of an experiment is to learn something you didn't know. Based on what you learn, you can then make a more educated guess for the next experiment. Often the result of an experiment is not one right answer but ten new questions. When you adopt a scientist's mindset, you become naturally curious. By focusing on becoming *less* wrong, you relieve yourself of the pressure to be right, and you can spend your time learning.

A practical way to become more open is to avoid using absolute language like "always," "never," "every," "all the time," and other similar phrases. Business development is complex. When you oversimplify a complex situation, you may become more rigid in your thinking. According to Professor Grant, just acknowledging complexity can help you be more openminded. Using phrases like "It depends" or "I could be off the mark here" or "based on the information I've seen so far," you express the multifaceted nature of most situations to both yourself and your clients, colleagues, or peers. These statements demonstrate one hallmark of an open mind: the willingness to change it.

Expressed Humility Statements
- I am willing to learn from others.
- I am open to others' ideas.
- I am open to advice.

American author and pastor Rick Warren sums it up well: "Humility is not thinking less of yourself; it is thinking of yourself less."[20] We need to keep that in mind every day, and in every client interaction—it's about them, not us. When our ego tricks us into thinking it is about us, and we begin to believe it, that's when we, like Icarus, begin to fly a bit closer to the Sun. As soon as we convince ourselves we won't be consumed by our ego, we most certainly will, so remain vigilant. Don't take any opportunity for granted. Treat every potential piece of business like the most important deal you want to close. We are prone to be proud, but we can actively cultivate humility to prevent a demise of our own making. By being more confident in our ability to figure things out, and less confident in knowing what's best, we set ourselves up with a rainmaker mindset that will lead to both short-term and long-term success.

Self-Reflection Questions

1. What am I doing today to prevent my ego from becoming over-inflated?

2. Can I articulate the difference between confidence and ego? Do I see myself as valuable or invaluable?

3. Which element of humility would I benefit the most from cultivating: being more objective about my abilities and limitations, being more appreciative of others' strengths and contributions, or being more open to feedback, ideas, and others' opinions?

4. How can I be a fan of others? What are ways I can help other people look good and feel successful?

5. When I review my activities over the past week and month, am I still hungry for business development, or have I become complacent?

6. What words or phrases can I remove from my vocabulary to show I'm more of a "scientist," striving to find answers, and less of a preacher, prosecutor, or politician, who are rigid in their beliefs?

END OF PART I:
Mindset Matters

As Roger Kneebone, the author of *Expert* introduced in Chapter 1, notes, "Becoming expert is about identity, about becoming a taxidermist, a tailor, or a computer programmer; not just being able to do the things those people do."[1] Put another way, identity matters, and your identity is not just a function of what you do, but how you think. You want to *become* a rainmaker, not just perform rainmaking activities. Your business development success will therefore be a by-product of inhabiting the rainmaker mindset, a shift from thinking *about* rainmakers to thinking *as* a rainmaker. This shift brings on sustained change. If you just learned rainmaking strategies and tactics without being eagerly dedicated, authentically open, consistently client-focused, realistically optimistic, and confidently humble, your execution would be off the mark. All five of these attitudes are mindsets in themselves, but when woven together, they create the overall rainmaker mindset.

When you're *eagerly dedicated*, you'll make the leap into business development without the mental shackles of hesitation and doubt that make it difficult to succeed. Once you've decided to make business development your main function, being *authentically open* will fast track your development through the growth mindset and leverage who you are as your differentiator. As you start to find your inner rainmaker, you'll become more relevant and trustworthy to your clients by being *consistently client-focused*. This trust will help them see you as their assistant buyer, instead of another salesperson. As you continue to engage prospects and clients, your *realistic optimism* will help you persevere until you succeed, no matter how big or frequent the setback. Lastly, by showing *confident humility*, you'll thwart your ego's ability to sabotage your success, both in the short-term and long-term.

As you read Part II, keep thinking about the five foundational pillars of the rainmaker mindset highlighted above. As you continue to shift your thinking to that of a rainmaker, you'll be in a more effective frame of mind to take advantage of the concrete strategies for building your book of business.

PART

II

Strategies

When delivering work to your clients, you know what you need to do at any given moment. Building your book of business is different. On top of juggling your existing responsibilities—delivery, client service, internal team management—when selling your work, you need to think about your potential contacts, decide which to pursue, network, maintain existing relationships, build new ones, create thought leadership . . . the list goes on. It's easy to wonder, "Where do I even start?"

To make the most of your business development efforts, you'll need solid rainmaking strategies to complement your rainmaker mindset. While building your book of business, you will find yourself in one of three scenarios with your prospects, clients, and influencers in your network:

1. **When you're searching for a real need:** Here, you'll be reaching out to individuals who may or may not know you, and who haven't yet shared their needs with you.

2. **When a need presents itself:** In this scenario, you'll be connecting with existing or new contacts who have come to you with a concrete need they think you can help address.

3. **When you're uncovering additional needs:** Once you're hired, this is the scenario in which you look to expand your business with your existing client.

For each scenario, you'll need different strategies designed to help you successfully uncover opportunities to support your client. Since that's the case, Part II is designed as a practical playbook to help you quickly identify the best strategy and the next business development step for any prospect or client you're pursuing.

The key is matching the right strategy with the right scenario. If a prospect hasn't come to you with a concrete need, reaching out and trying to pitch and close them will likely lead to disappointment for you, and even worse, annoyance for them. Alternatively, you may have a longstanding client who knows you well and respects your work but isn't aware you can be helpful in another context. If that's the case, you'll want to shift your focus from pure relationship building to increasing awareness of your other offerings. These strategies will also help you switch gears more quickly as you simultaneously manage different contacts in different scenarios, or as your contacts move among the three scenarios. For example, you might finish an engagement with an existing client, and after some time passes, they move from the third scenario back into the first one.

Instead of the traditional sales funnel, this scenario-based approach is more practical for juggling the wide-ranging responsibilities of a rainmaker. With strong strategies in place for each scenario, you'll be able to map out where your contacts are at any point in time and follow up with the appropriate activities, as detailed in Chapters 6–8. Just like the questions at the end of each chapter in Part I are designed to help you shift into the rainmaker mindset, the metrics at the end of each chapter in Part II will help you see how well you're implementing the given strategy. Having concrete strategies will allow you to be more intentional in your business development approach and guide the tactics you'll learn in Part III.

CHAPTER

6

Mining for Gold: When You're Searching for a Real Need

Chapter 6: Mining for Gold: When You're Searching for a Real Need

While vacationing in the Caribbean, Michael Haugen, a partner at ghSMART, a Chicago-based leadership advisory firm, was looking forward to some well-deserved R&R with his wife and young daughter. On the way there, as they waited for their flight, a family with kids sat nearby, and they struck up a casual conversation. After landing at their Caribbean destination, they all realized they were staying at the same resort.

The two families hung out together multiple times that week, as their kids were all about the same age. Haugen and his family mostly spent time with the mom and their kids, learning that the dad was frequently on business calls, even during vacation. The times Haugen did see the other dad, he would keep the conversation light, not wanting to take up even more of the other dad's scarce vacation time talking about work or reminding him of any worries he'd left behind on the mainland. After the week was up, and they went to say goodbye, Haugen and the other dad swapped business cards so the families could keep in touch. Turns out this dad was the CEO and Chairman of a major retail chain in the US; he invited Haugen to meet with him next time he was in town.

Haugen couldn't believe his good luck. Still, landing business with this CEO's company was by no means a done deal. The two men kept in touch. Haugen let the CEO know whenever he was in town, and each time the CEO did indeed invite Haugen to meet with him. Haugen recalls, "I don't know how many different trips I made on my dime, just to chat, to meet his head of HR, COO, CFO." But it paid off. By making contact, staying in touch, and consistently following up, Haugen developed a real relationship with the CEO, his company, and his colleagues. When the time was right, and it turned out they could use ghSMART's services, Haugen was the first person they called. Since the CEO and Haugen already knew, liked, and trusted each other, they were happy to work together, and the company became a big client for Haugen and his firm.

Opportunities can come from anywhere. Many of your business development efforts will start with people who are not actively coming to you with opportunities. When you're searching for new business, your goal is to build relationships, so you are top of mind when an opportunity arises. In Haugen's case, by being friendly and personable, he made a social connection that paid off professionally. But after that initial contact, he still had to put in the work to develop that relationship until a real opportunity came up. In some cases, being top of mind may be enough to find a concrete need; in other situations, you might trigger a need by sharing insights, best practices, and new offerings with your contacts. You'll want to take a purposeful approach to decide who best to pursue, and how, while maximizing both the quantity of opportunities and the quality of your pursuit.

Decide Who to Pursue: Your Ideal Connections

When building your book of business, you want to prioritize the names on your outreach list by how likely they are to work with you. As a rainmaker, your time and energy are limited. Don't waste your resources reaching out to people who probably aren't a good match or interested in working with you (or even responding to you). One way to focus your business development efforts is to create an Ideal Connections list and organize these contacts into four distinct groups:

1. Existing and former clients
2. "Sweet spot" prospects

3. Influencers
4. Supporters

You'll want to consistently increase the number of contacts and interactions you have in the first two groups, existing and former clients and your "sweet spot" prospects. Once you exhaust your touchpoints there, move to the next two groups, influencers and supporters.

Existing and Former Clients

People who have hired you before are likely to hire you again. You probably keep close tabs on your existing clients, but you'll want to give former clients high priority as well when building your Ideal Connections list. They know what you're capable of, and they have already trusted you to work with them. If your existing clients are mostly your more senior colleagues' contacts, mine your firm's past relationships to begin building your own client base. Check to see if your firm has a list of former clients who haven't been contacted in a while. You can also investigate inactive accounts of your seasoned or retired colleagues. If you uncover dormant contacts, ask your manager or the appropriate colleague if you can add them to your Ideal Connections list. It is easy to lose track of former buyers, especially if they've stopped buying because they brought your service in-house, lost their budget, or have moved to another organization. Approaching former buyers can be an extremely valuable activity, as they can offer introductions or hire you again once their current firms, or future employers, are looking for your services.

"Sweet Spot" Prospects

The next group on your Ideal Connections list should be potential buyers who may not know you yet but fit into your "sweet spot."

Your sweet spot prospects are those people who would value your services based on what they do, what they're looking for, and what you bring to the table. These individuals will likely take your call because of your client list, past deals, and reputation in their industry. To identify these sweet spot prospects, analyze your existing client base, noting similarities between the companies that consistently hire you or your firm. Next, target similar prospects based on industry, function, company size, growth rate, or other defining attributes. You can also seek out prospects who likely experience the problems you're great at solving. Ask yourself who would find value in your expertise, relationships, industry and institutional knowledge, geographic reach, company size and structure, or way of doing business.

Influencers

The third group of contacts to place on your Ideal Connections list are the "influencers," people who can lead you to a buyer or sway their decision to hire you. Often, they are your prospects' advisors and insiders. When you build strong relationships with members of this group, they can help you navigate the decision-making process, prepare you for key meetings, and share feedback from those meetings. Think about the players who were a part of your previous deals that have seen you in action. These could include other senior executives, key team members, accountants, lawyers, consultants, or board directors. By cultivating a strong relationship with these influencers, you're increasing the chances that they will recommend you or inform you of opportunities.

Supporters

The fourth and final group on your Ideal Connections list will be those people who support your success, but who are not part of the first three groups. They may be friends, relatives, colleagues, or professional contacts open to helping you build a relationship with one of your prospects (sometimes your supporters' firm ends up needing your services as well). They may be willing to share information and advice, make introductions, and even refer business. If they work at your prospects' organization, they might help you navigate the organization's structure and understand its main priorities. Find ways to stay connected with your supporters to help you cast a wide net—you never know where opportunities may arise. Follow them on social media so they stay on your radar. If your firm has a mailing list, ask if they'd like to be added to it so they can remain in the loop on what's happening at your firm.

Find the Right Fit

Once you come up with your initial Ideal Connections list, further refine this list by their fit to you and your firm. The better the fit, the higher your chances of being hired. Like any successful long-term relationship, you and your Ideal Connections should both find working together beneficial. Your value to them, and their value to you, will come from your mutual ability to help each other reach your professional and personal goals. For most professionals, they assess the value of working with a particular client based on three elements: the potential revenue from that client, affiliation with that client's brand, and the chance to further develop one's own professional skills.

You'll likely weigh all three factors in deciding if it's worthwhile to pursue a particular client. If a client can generate a significant amount of revenue for you, you may not care if their brand enhances yours. Similarly, if a particular client has a project that won't generate much revenue but provides the opportunity to help you build out a new offering to other clients, you may decide to take the engagement.

In addition to the potential value, you'll want to consider the *likelihood* of receiving that value. For example, if you're only working with a client because they can enhance your brand, but they won't allow you to use their name in your marketing materials, you may want to reassess. These considerations are all a question of whether these clients will offer you enough value potential to reach your goals.

Keep in mind, though, revenue, brand impact, and learning potential may not be the only criteria to determine whether you should work with a specific client. You might also consider whether you and your company's culture and values mesh with your potential client's. There are some organizations you may decide not to pursue based on their business practices and industry, while you may favor others based on factors like their mission or geography. For example, some of my clients refuse to work with tobacco companies, and others lean toward socially-responsible organizations looking to reduce carbon emissions. There are also working styles to consider. Some clients might expect you to be on call 24/7 via Slack, while you prefer to only work Monday–Friday, 9 am to 5 pm, and keep in touch by weekly video call check-ins.

When the fit in any of these areas is off, you won't serve your clients well, and the lackluster outcome will hurt your reputation. To help you be more aware of your preferences, think about your best clients and reflect on why you enjoy working with them. As you review your Ideal Connections list, keep these preferences in mind. If there isn't a great match, you may want to take them off your list.

Another consideration in regard to fit is the size of the company. In general, it takes a similar amount of effort to build a relationship with an individual buyer at Amazon versus one at a small e-commerce company. Although large organizations typically have more revenue potential and brand cachet, the probability of winning a deal may be lower. They're likely working with an incumbent, making competition for their business fierce. Bigger companies also have resources to bring your type of expertise in-house. With those facts in mind, you may have a better chance winning a deal with smaller companies, *but* the total dollar value might be low for the effort and time you put in. You may have less competition with a smaller client as well, but you'll also have fewer opportunities to grow that account once you've established yourself with them.

Still, smaller companies can help you rack up some quick wins and hit your short-term revenue goals. They can also give you a chance to sharpen your rainmaking skills in a lower-stakes setting. Landing a deal, no matter the size of the client, will be a confidence booster that you can carry into your pursuit of larger companies. Also, people tend to move around between companies, so someone you work with today at a small firm may end up at a much larger one in the future. The more connections you make, the more opportunities you can potentially uncover.

When building your book of business—especially when you're just starting out—you don't want to be overly selective in your approach. Well-meaning advice like, "You want quality, not quantity" or "Work smarter, not harder," may be sound, but when you're developing as a rainmaker, this guidance could work against you. If you're too selective, you might prematurely limit your pool of contacts. In an effort to seek out "quality" or to work "smarter," you may spend more time reorganizing your prospecting list than actually reaching out to your prospects.

Maximize the *quantity* of your business development activity early on. To fit this into your already busy schedule, you'll want to purposefully shift more time to business development while making sure your existing client engagements are taken care of. (Tactics on managing this shift can be found in Chapter 12.) The more time you spend on business development, the more opportunities you'll have to refine your skills and discover the activities that work best for you. In time, you can better decide what "quality" looks like for you, your style of selling, and your set of clients.

The strategy in this first scenario is to identify your Ideal Connections, refine the list based on fit, and advance the relationship with these individuals. If you've just started building your book of business, focus on expanding your Ideal Connections list. You can begin by searching your company's internal client database. You might find additional names by searching for titles of existing or former buyers on LinkedIn. For example, "Treasurer at XYZ company." If you don't have a buyer's current contact information, you might use ZoomInfo and other B2B databases. If you have a personal contact at your target company, ask that person to help you navigate their company's org structure. Your strategy is to identify and focus on the *person* who is responsible for hiring your type of expertise. Once you've identified specific names of potential buyers of your services and a way to reach them, it's time to make contact.

Advance the Relationship

With your Ideal Connections, it's up to you to make the first move and advance the relationship. The further along your relationship, the more willing they will be to share their needs and consider working with you. Depending on the stage of the relationship, you will employ different strategies to deepen trust and uncover a real opportunity, as detailed in Figure 6.1.

Based on Figure 6.1, pick any contact from your Ideal Connections list and decide which stage they are in. As shown, for each stage, there are specific actions you can take to help you move to the following one. You'll typically be in different stages

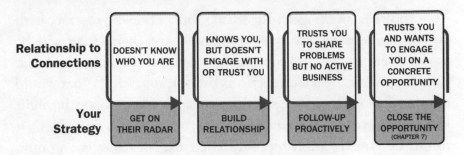

Relationship to Connections	DOESN'T KNOW WHO YOU ARE	KNOWS YOU, BUT DOESN'T ENGAGE WITH OR TRUST YOU	TRUSTS YOU TO SHARE PROBLEMS BUT NO ACTIVE BUSINESS	TRUSTS YOU AND WANTS TO ENGAGE YOU ON A CONCRETE OPPORTUNITY
Your Strategy	GET ON THEIR RADAR	BUILD RELATIONSHIP	FOLLOW-UP PROACTIVELY	CLOSE THE OPPORTUNITY (CHAPTER 7)

FIGURE 6.1 The Right Strategy for the Right Stage

of your relationship with different Ideal Connections. The key is understanding what to do next, depending on that stage, and remaining proactive. Rainmaking is not order taking; it's the ability to make business happen. If you sit around hoping clients will come to you when they have a need, you'll probably be waiting a long time.

1. Doesn't Know Who You Are: Get on Their Radar

There will be people on your Ideal Connections list who don't know who you are or who may not remember you. Your goal with these individuals is to attract their attention. But since most people are already attention-strapped, you need to give them a compelling reason to respond to you. There are three main reasons your Ideal Connections will engage with you in this stage:

1. They have an immediate need you can help solve and are open to exploring new resources.
2. They were asked by someone in their network to speak with you, and are willing to do that person a favor, or they feel compelled to speak with you because you share a common affiliation.
3. They feel that getting to know you will be personally beneficial.

You're trying to get your Ideal Connections to interact with you. If that interaction proves valuable for them, they will be more open to developing a relationship with you. For each person on your Ideal Connections list, ask yourself, "What would get this person to want to speak to me again?" For some, it might be access to your knowledge, network, or expertise. For others, it might be your relationship with their executives or a common interest or affiliation. By highlighting your value or a common connection, you're more likely to get a response from the other person.

Get the Timing Right

Although ideally, we would reach out to a client at just the right point when they need our services, we can't know or control that timing. We can, however, understand their buying habits and broadly anticipate their needs. Assess whether your service is one that your Ideal Connections need constantly, periodically, or infrequently. If your service is needed constantly (like training), cold outreach efforts at any time may be worthwhile since you're likely to contact someone who is actively engaging this service. If potential clients hire your service periodically (like audit and tax services), you'll want to leverage your supporters at those companies to guide you on their buying cycle.

If you're in a business where clients hire you infrequently (like mergers and acquisitions or anti-trust litigation), you may want to develop relationships with intermediaries and influencers. Prospects who infrequently buy your type of services may not have a great deal of experience vetting your expertise. Also, even if they hire you, they may not engage you again, meaning they may be less interested in building a direct relationship with you. To find a resource to meet an infrequent need, they are more prone to asking their existing network for a recommendation. In such cases, random cold outreach will likely fail. Instead, try to stay in touch with influencers so they can pull you in when they hear a need.

You may also think about the general trends or trigger events that favor your service. For example, if you are an M&A advisor, you may target companies who are in an industry that is quickly consolidating. Depending on your service, you could keep an eye out for a bankruptcy filing, a new strategic initiative, or a cybersecurity incident. It's not easy to get timing right but stepping into your potential client's perspective can increase your chances of getting a response.

Practical Tip

Set up a Google alert for each of your Ideal Connections, their respective organizations, and relevant trigger events. By getting a digest of news related to your Ideal Connections, you'll not only have a reminder to reach out, but potentially a reason to as well.

Get an Introduction

Review your network for individuals connected to your Ideal Connections or who work at the companies you're pursuing. Ask them if they might be willing to introduce you or share information that may be helpful in warming up your outreach. When asking for an introduction, consider language along the following lines:

> "Janet, it was great seeing you last month. I see that you're connected with [Ideal Connection], and I was wondering if you would be open to introducing us. We recently delivered work for [similar group] that I thought might be interesting to share with [Ideal Connection]. If it's helpful, I can draft a brief intro note for you to adjust."

Note the difference between this suggested language and just asking your contact, "Can you introduce me to [Ideal Connection]?" In the earlier example, you've done the groundwork and are just asking your contact for a boost. You're also not asking them to do all of the legwork.

If this individual works at one of your potential clients, but you're not sure whether they know your Ideal Connection, you might take a slightly different approach:

> "Janet, it was great seeing you last month. Do you know [Ideal Connection] by any chance? He works on the finance team, and I was hoping to invite him to one of our firm's upcoming events for comptrollers. If you don't know him, do you have any advice on the best way to reach him?"

If you sense a person is uncomfortable introducing you, ask if they would be open to you referencing their name when you reach out to the potential contact. You're more likely to get a response if you reference a name the contact knows. The email subject, "Janet Paine suggested I reach out to you," will be opened more often than "Open to connecting about professional skills training?" If your contact would prefer to be left out of your outreach altogether, give them an out by telling them you can reach out directly without mentioning their name.

Go Direct: Cold Outreach

What if you don't know anyone who can introduce you to the specific person you want to connect with on your Ideal Connections list? If members of your network are unable to help you, the fastest way to get on that person's radar is to reach out directly, instead of waiting for a "warm" introduction. Compared to warm outreach, cold outreach has a lower probability of getting a response, but if you don't already have a strong book of business, lower probability is better than *no* probability. When you have no existing relationship with an Ideal Connection, reaching out cold may still lead to some success. A benchmark study of 488 buyers across 25 industries found that 82 percent of buyers accept meetings with sellers who proactively reach out to them if they see a need for the service, can likely find the budget, and feel they will gain value from the interaction.[1] Cold outreach helps you sharpen your pitch and overcome the anxiety of speaking to strangers. Think of it like a fire extinguisher: You rarely need to use it, but when you have to, you want to make sure you know how.

There will also be times when the people you cold call will respond simply because they are nice, or they've had to do cold outreach themselves and can empathize with your situation. (Salespeople are always a good first contact when trying to make headway at a company—they may feel for you, and they'll know who to best connect you with.) Some of your Ideal Connections will at least hear you out, and if they think developing a relationship with you might be worthwhile down the line, there's a chance they will be open to reconnecting.

When it comes to cold calling, remember these simple tips for maximum effect:

- **Make it quick.** Know what you want to say and be transparent up front. Cold outreach only takes a few seconds when people don't respond and typically a few minutes when they do. Anything longer means the conversation is going well.

- **Stay conversational and confident.** Speak with a matter-of-fact and friendly tone like you would to a fellow business-person, colleague, or peer. When you sound tentative, salesy, or overly deferential, you make the other person uncomfortable and less likely to engage.

- **Be prepared, bold, and respectful.** It's scary to reach out to someone you don't know, and even more frightening when they actually respond. Practice so you are ready for any reaction. And stay respectful and positive; if they are not interested, then disengage politely—there is no need to try to convince them in the moment or be impolite.

- **Warm it up as much as possible.** Reference something familiar to increase the response rate. You might mention that you're a fellow alumnus, congratulate them on a notable accomplishment, or bring up a recent article they wrote or a talk they gave.

The cold outreach template in Table 6.1 can help you get started.

Table 6.1   Cold Outreach Template

Introduce yourself
- Say, "Hi [decision-maker name], it's (your name) from [your firm]. We're a [type of company]."

Share relevant info to warm up call
- Referral, affiliation, common connection, trigger event, insight
- Ask, "Is now a good time?"
  - If "yes," go to next bullet
  - If "no," ask, "When might be a good time to call back?"

Explain the reason for calling and share value for connecting
- Calling to set up a meeting, invite to an event, follow-up on email
- Be ready to engage in a conversation if the other person has time or manage the common objections (discussed in Chapter 11)

End call (be ready to leave voicemail if applicable)

An example of the template in action might look something like this:

Introduce self and share relevant info

- "Hi John. It's Robert Chen from Exec|Comm. We're a communication skills training company. Jude Singh suggested I reach out to you since you run training at XYZ Company. Is now a good time?"

- John responds, "Actually, I thought you were my 2:00 call. What can I do for you?"

Explain the reason for calling and share value for connecting

- "Sorry if I have caught you at a bad time, I'll be quick. Your colleague Jude Singh thought it might be helpful for you to learn about my firm as a resource as you explore revamping your professional skills curriculum. I'm glad to call back later in the week if you're open to a short call."

- John replies, "Well, we're on the phone now, and I have two minutes, why don't you tell me what kind of services you provide?"

- "Thanks John, we [share value you can offer and learn about John's focus]. Would you be open to continuing the conversation later this month?"

- "Let me connect you with someone on my team," John says, "and they can set it up."

- "Thank you, I really appreciate it."

End call

To avoid sounding robotic, or as if you're reading off of a script, you can condense your word-for-word script into a keyword outline. You'll see in Figure 6.2 what an outline might look like for the script above.

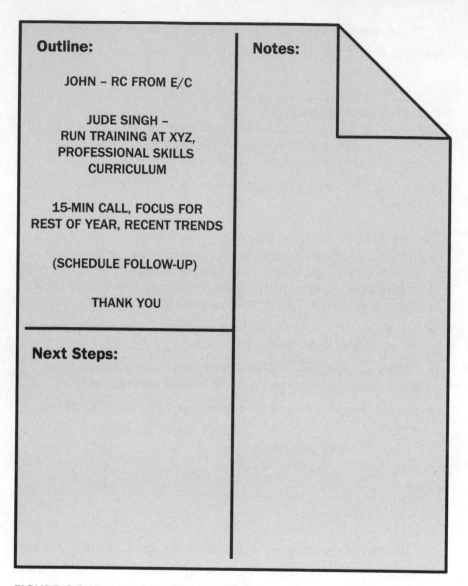

FIGURE 6.2 Keyword Outline Template

By using this key word outline, you'll stay organized while remaining conversational. As you see in Figure 6.2, you can have your outline on the same page you take your notes. An outline also allows you to dive quickly back into outreach if you get pulled away by other work. Remember to keep your requests short and specific and maintain a positive tone throughout, no matter how the other person responds.

Cold outreach rewards creativity. Go beyond just looking for common connections on LinkedIn. For example, as Spanx founder and CEO Sara Blakely built her shapewear empire, she found humor to be a great way to break through the frozen waters of cold calling and get people's attention. Early on, she targeted a buyer at Neiman Marcus by sending a shoebox containing a high-heel and a hand-written note reading, "Just trying to get my foot in the door. Can I have a few minutes of your time?"[2] It worked, but if Blakely kept sending her prospects shoes, it would have likely lost its impact and felt gimmicky, stale, and uninspired. Also, getting attention is different from keeping attention. Blakely's success didn't come from getting the attention of Neiman Marcus, it came from keeping her buyer's attention by sharing a valuable product. For cold outreach, you need both the sizzle and the steak.

2. Knows You but Doesn't Engage with or Trust You: Build a Relationship

When your Ideal Connections are lukewarm to you, or keep you at arm's length, you'll want to focus on deepening your relationship with them. They will engage more frequently with you when they feel they will benefit from the interaction. Look for ways to position yourself as the person who will help them accomplish their professional and personal goals. Maybe that means sharing a resource with them that's aligned with an initiative they're working on or introducing them to someone they might benefit from meeting. Perhaps it's figuring out a way to take some work off their plate. In essence, you're trying to make their lives easier, leaving them with either a positive interaction, a positive outcome, or both. Someone who gains something of value when they interact with you will likely interact with you again.

When speaking with your Ideal Connections, keep an ear out for the other person's aspirations. Michael Haugen, the partner from ghSMART mentioned earlier in the chapter, suggests using a "past, present, future" framework to naturally guide the conversation in this direction. He explains, "As you are talking to somebody and you want them to start sharing, ask them about their story. . . 'How did you get to this job? Where did you grow up? What did you study?' These questions get you toward understanding the trajectory of their lives." Once you cover the past, you'll want to transition forward to the present.

"The present is all about what they are focused on today. 'What are the things that keep you up at night? What are the current issues you face?'" The future questions follow. "Ask them 'What's next for you in your career? What would be a homerun for your next role, your next company, or next investment?'" When it all comes together, the real opportunities present themselves.

> "If you can get people talking and comfortable on the past side, then seamlessly transition into understanding where they are today—without making it feel awkward and weird—then you get to a level of trust in which you ask, 'What's next?' People will open up in ways you would never expect."

By following this framework, a holistic view of your Ideal Connections, and what matters most to them, will emerge. And the more you understand their priorities, the more likely you can find opportunities to help them reach their goals.

Once you've made a solid connection, regularly check in with your Ideal Connections. When you do touch base, ask how they're doing and offer something of value. You might share an insight or best practice or introduce your Ideal Connection to someone they want to meet. Be ready to also talk about what you're working on, since it's likely they will ask you what you're up to. When possible, discuss recent experiences relevant to their issues and goals, pulling them further into the conversation and getting them to think about how you might add more value for them. Still, pleasant conversations are not enough. Your main goal is not only to keep their permission to stay in touch, but to deepen your relationship. The best way to do that is to escalate commitment.

Escalate Commitment

Relationships develop when both sides take a risk to make a commitment together.[3] If that commitment is kept and both sides benefit, the relationship deepens. Each party becomes more interdependent, creating a willingness to take bigger risks and make bigger commitments to each other. For example, when a decision-maker commits to listen to you for a few minutes when you call them, if you say something of value, they may increase their commitment by agreeing to meet with you in-person to share their specific needs. When you meet with them, if you show you can help with what they're looking to achieve, they may commit to bringing you back to speak with their senior stakeholders. If you do well in that interaction, they will escalate their commitment again, hiring you to run a pilot engagement. If the pilot is successful, they may be comfortable signing a multi-year deal together. And so forth and so on. These escalating commitments, when met, lead to loyalty and a desire to preserve the relationship.[4]

Before you can escalate commitment, though, you need to secure the first commitment by making an appropriate ask of your Ideal Connection. Ask for a call, ask for a meeting, ask to read a report, ask to attend an event, ask to be considered on your prospect's preferred supplier list, ask them to join your advisory council. These are all easier said than done. Making an ask can be uncomfortable. Some people hesitate to ask because they don't want to be rejected, while others don't make an ask because they feel like they're begging. Instead, see asking as the first step to launching a meaningful relationship. The other person can still say, "no," but let them decide. Don't say "no" to yourself by not asking. Research shows we typically underestimate the willingness of strangers to say "yes" because we recognize the burden of them saying "yes," but not the cost to them when they say "no."[5] People don't feel good about saying "no" to someone else, so you may have a better chance than you think. You won't know what's possible unless you ask.

When making the ask, give the person an out so they will continue to engage with you in the future. If you corner someone into saying, "yes," they might do so once, but afterward, they'll try to avoid you at all costs. (Surprise, surprise: This is not a good strategy for long-term success.) See every ask you make as a request, not a demand. If they say "yes," great! If they say "no," it's not personal—the commitment you're asking them to make is just not interesting or comfortable for them right now. Find another smaller ask when the time is right. For example, if they decline your offer to meet with them, you might ask if they would like to attend a complimentary workshop next month. Once you find the right ask that creates the initial commitment, overdeliver on that commitment so you can escalate to the next potentially bigger commitment.

3. Trusts You to Share Problems but No Active Opportunity: Follow-Up Proactively

As much as your Ideal Connections might like you, they probably don't think about you often unless they have a problem you can solve. Even when they have a need for your services, your name may not readily come to mind. Since that's the case, your success will come from consistent follow-up. Every time you touch base, you're refreshing their memory of you. By being top of mind to your Ideal Connections, you may be considered for new opportunities, either for right then, or in the future. In each follow-up, you have three distinct ways to uncover a concrete opportunity: by learning more about what your buyer might need, raising awareness of potential needs, and positioning yourself to be in the "right place at the right time."

Learn More about Your Buyer

Though you'll know a lot about your Ideal Connections at this point in your relationship, you can always learn more about their buying preferences and their evolving goals when you touch base with them. You might, for example, find out about a new strategic initiative you could help with but weren't considered for because your contact didn't realize the full scope of your capabilities. One of my colleagues at Exec|Comm was always tapped by a specific client for one-on-one executive coaching, but nothing else. After a few years into their relationship, during a routine check-in, the client mentioned they were requesting a proposal for a global leadership development program from a few of our competitors. My colleague politely asked why they hadn't considered our firm. "Oh," said the client, "do you do that? I didn't realize you had facilitators outside of the US." By checking in and mutually sharing an update, you may uncover a potential opportunity. As shown in Figure 6.1, at that point, it's time to move on to the next scenario, detailed in Chapter 7.

Raise Awareness of a Need

Another way to uncover a real opportunity is to show your prospects a need they might not realize they have, but upon hearing it, immediately recognize the value in addressing it. One of Exec|Comm's technology consulting clients would regularly send their clients detailed use cases for applying automation to corporate functions like HR. By sharing specifics around a use case, they not only provided interesting information, but raised their clients' awareness about a service they might be missing out on.

Share ideas your Ideal Connections may not have considered—what are similar companies doing or broader trends your Ideal Connections are not talking about? For example, if an industry, like retail, is moving toward digitization, you may approach mid-market brick-and-mortar retailers to suggest ways they should be thinking about this change. By raising their awareness of an unfulfilled need that they recognize is worth addressing, you may now have a concrete opportunity, which again moves you to the next scenario, detailed in Chapter 7.

Be in the Right Place at the Right Time

Though the idea of "being in the right place at the right time" traditionally relies on luck, if you put yourself in a place frequently enough, you might just bump into the right time. One of my clients loves tennis. She buys tickets to the US Open every year and invites her Ideal Connections who are tennis fans as well. She'll bring different connections to each game, giving her a chance to spend time, share a fun experience, and deepen the relationship with them individually. She's mentioned that even when they can't make it, they think of her when the US Open is on. By leveraging her unique interests, and those of her Ideal Connections, she creates opportunities to further build relationships. You might host a networking happy hour, recommend an interesting book or article, or schedule a workout session together. One of my colleagues sends orchids to their clients who they know will appreciate them. Every time their client sees the flowers, my colleague's name likely comes to mind. (Hint: Orchids and green plants last longer than cut flowers.)

Sometimes it's okay to ping your Ideal Connection to just check in on them. You don't always need to lead with specific business value as the main reason for connecting. They may find value just speaking with a good listener (people pay therapists for this all the time) or someone they connect with well. Look for interesting people you would want to build a relationship with, even if you don't end up working together. Haugen echoes this idea when he says, "At the end of the day, if all you do is meet a cool person, make some good introductions for them, and provide them value, that's a win. You don't always have to get a contract, and often if you push too hard with an executive, you'll decrease your chances of success."

You don't need to call the same contact every month. Just stay in touch in meaningful ways. The idea is to reach out consistently—without being annoying—until the other person responds. Even when they don't reply, they may see or hear your name, and that might be enough to remind them of you. For most of your Ideal Connections, a minimum quarterly cadence may be enough, along with events-driven check-ins like birthdays, promotions, or notable news. If you don't have a relevant check-in, create one. Host an event that's interesting for your Ideal Connections or schedule a trip to their city. When you consistently stay top of mind, you'll find that you'll be in the right place at the right time more often. In Chapter 7, you'll learn to close the potential opportunities that arise.

Create a System to Follow Up

As a rainmaker, you will be pulled in many directions, so it's important to have a system to consistently stay active in building and strengthening relationships and filling your business development pipeline. This system should be easy to access and take as little time as possible to update. The goal is to help you quickly figure out whom you need to reach out to when you switch back into your business development mode. Some use a paper planner or an excel spreadsheet, while others may leverage a Google doc or Customer Relationship Management (CRM) software. No matter what system you use, you'll want to include the following elements:

1. Account and contact name. (Who?)
2. The next step, last discussion topic, or reason for outreach. (What?)
3. Date for your next follow-up. (When?)

If you decide to use a system, it may be helpful to rank your Ideal Connections from 1 through 4, with 1 being the highest priority:

1. Existing and Former clients
2. "Sweet Spot" Prospects
3. Influencers
4. Supporters

As your Ideal Connections' situations change, you can update their ranking. By having a system that allows you to quickly see the next step for each Ideal Connection, you'll, hopefully, never again have to wonder, "Where do I start?"

Metrics

Below are some metrics that will help you assess your effectiveness and consistency in reaching out to and advancing your relationship with your Ideal Connections. Metrics aren't for everyone, but if you do decide to use these, choose those that are most relevant to you and your business. Whenever possible, find a way to automatically compile these metrics so you don't have to spend too much time putting them all together.

Metric	How to Calculate	Implications/Application
Existing Buyers	Count existing buyers	The more existing buyers you have, the stronger the base for your book of business. You can tap this group for referrals, further expanding your revenue potential.
Potential and Former Buyers	Count potential and former buyers you've already contacted and would respond to your outreach	You've already connected with these buyers, but they have not hired you recently or ever. They have the budget but are not spending it with you. You can use this number to measure your business development progress even if your revenue is not increasing.
Influencers	Count C-suite executives, advisors, or other influencers you've connected with and who would respond to your outreach	These individuals can pull you into deals, influence decision-makers, or introduce you to potential buyers. If you have too many Ideal Connections, you might track just the influencers who have already brought you in on business.

Metric	How to Calculate	Implications/Application
Sales Activity Metrics	Count sales-related activity per month: • sales interactions • sales emails sent • speaking engagements • networking events	These metrics show you the quantity of your business development efforts. Your firm may have benchmark activity numbers you'll want to hit or exceed. If you have a clear way of qualifying your prospects, then you might want to only track sales-related activities with qualified prospects.
Revenue/ Activity Ratio	$$\frac{\text{Total Annual Revenue}}{\text{Total Sales Activities}}$$	This measure helps you gauge the quality of your activities. Each year, you'll want to increase your revenue/activity ratio, which shows your average deal size getting bigger. As you improve your skills, you should be generating more revenue per activity.
Average Client Size	Client size can be determined by: • Annual revenue or net income • # of employees • Year-over-year growth rate • Growth rate compared to peers • Industry ranking	You'll want the "right" clients for you and your services. Ideally, you'll want clients big enough so your relationships and wins within the organization will further increase your chances of winning other deals at the organization. To increase this metric, start shedding smaller clients as you land bigger ones.

Opportunity Knocks: When a Need Presents Itself

Chapter 7: Opportunity Knocks: When a Need Presents Itself

When once asked by his daughter, who was five at the time, about what he does for a living, Mohamed Kande, the Global Advisory Leader for PwC introduced in Chapter 3, told her he's a consultant. Cocking her head to one side with a questioning look, she asked what that meant. Kande replied, "I'm basically a doctor for companies."

It's no wonder Kande views himself as such. Like doctors, professional service providers need both technical expertise and strong diagnostic abilities to understand how to best apply that expertise. Research by Professor Susan Fiske[1] mentioned in Chapter 3 shows that doctors are typically rated as high warmth and high competence. Further, doctors don't look to prove themselves. (Kande remarks, "When you go to the doctor, they never start by telling you where they went to school, or what they've done. They start by asking, 'How are you feeling?'") Nor are doctors overly deferential—instead, they garner respect. They also don't prescribe a solution until they've assessed the situation. (I believe prescription without assessment is usually called "malpractice.")

Most of these attributes should sound familiar. Like doctors, rainmakers deliver on their expertise. They are warm and competent and valued as trusted advisors. They instill confidence. They only suggest solutions after they've taken the time to more fully understand their clients' problems. Stepping into the medical doctor persona can therefore be a useful way to help you navigate your interactions when an opportunity presents itself. Once your prospects decide they have a need you can potentially address, your aim is to make it through their decision-making process and, if it's the right fit, be chosen as the resource to help them. Just like a skilled doctor, your goal is to figure out where it hurts and how to relieve the pain. In doing so, your potential opportunity will turn into a reality.

Close Potential Opportunities

You make an appointment with your doctor when you think they can help in some way. Most visits to the doctor follow a standard process. When you arrive, your doctor asks you what seems to be the problem. After your initial explanation, they follow up with a series of other questions. If necessary, they'll run some tests to gather more data. Once they feel they have enough information, they determine what's wrong. This could take a few minutes or a few weeks, but the result is hopefully the same—they diagnose the issue and give you their prognosis. Next, they identify what to do, and prescribe a solution to what ails you. This could come in the form of medication, surgery, or maybe just a recommendation for some exercise, healthy eating, and fresh air. Then they ask you, "What do you want to do?"

This process consists of three distinct steps: Assess, Diagnose, and Prescribe. As shown in Figure 7.1, as a rainmaker you'll take a similar approach with your prospects when they come to you with a need. (Although your existing clients may also come to you with an opportunity, the term "prospects" used

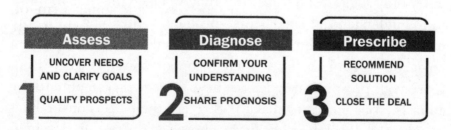

FIGURE 7.1 The Three-Step Assess, Diagnose, Prescribe Process

throughout this chapter refers to anyone with a prospective opportunity, whether or not you've worked with them before.)

You'll examine the issue your prospects are experiencing (Assess), identify what's wrong (Diagnose), and present solutions (Prescribe). These steps may happen in one meeting or across multiple interactions, but the goal is always the same for the rainmaker: closing the deal.

Step 1: Assess

When one of your prospects presents you with a concrete opportunity, your first step is to figure out what is going on in the situation and what help they might actually need. Your prospects may be coming to you for a variety of reasons. Again, think of them like patients: Some may be in great pain and need a solution right away, no matter the cost. Others may want to address bad habits that have finally caught up with them and explore options on how to turn things around before they get worse. And yet others may come to you because they've heard from a friend about a particular treatment that might be helpful for them to try. No matter their reason, your goal is to figure out why they've decided to see you and assess the situation so you can start diagnosing their issue.

Uncover Needs and Clarify Goals

When you begin your assessment, you'll ask some form of, "What's the purpose for your visit?" You might say, "As I was thinking about this meeting, I have a few questions I would love to ask you to better understand your situation." Then follow that statement up with, "What outcomes are you looking for? Why are they important to you? Why now?" If your prospect prefers a more formal tone, you might say, "The purpose for this meeting is to learn more about your goals and what you're looking to accomplish. These details will help determine whether we are the right resource for you. If we can be helpful, we're happy to share some ideas with you. If we end up not being the right fit, we may be able to refer you to someone else." If you sense your prospect might be more easygoing, you can give them a welcoming hello, warm smile, and say, "Tell us how we can help."

After your prospect shares more details about their situation, you'll want to resist the temptation to immediately steer the conversation toward your services. At this early stage, you probably don't know enough about their situation to be truly helpful. Proposing a solution too quickly also has an added risk of scaring off your prospect because you might propose something they may not be comfortable with yet. It's like your doctor prescribing medication or recommending surgery upfront after they ask you, "How are you feeling?" Even if they may be right, you're likely not going to have much confidence or comfort in their approach if it sounds like they're just taking your word for it and they're not really examining you.

Focus instead on diving deeper into the context of their situation, along with a sense of their desired outcome and their resources and constraints. Table 7.1 provides a list of questions you'll want to get answers to when you're interacting with your prospects. The questions in parenthesis are ones you likely won't be able to ask directly, but through your conversations, you may be able to piece together the answers.

Depending on your service, you may have different options to further examine the situation, like your doctor requesting and reviewing your bloodwork or X-rays. Though the conversation might be a good first step to assessing the issue, you may need to follow it up with deeper analysis. For example, you might perform a feasibility study by interviewing stakeholders, analyzing financial statements, or reviewing customer contracts. The more

Table 7.1 Questions to Assess Your Prospects' Situation

Three Key Assessment Factors	Questions
Context of the Situation	• Why now? • What have you tried? • What performance goal is driving this need? • How does this fit with your strategic goals? • (How will this initiative impact you in regard to reputation, promotion, recognition, or compensation?)
Desired Outcome	• What would you like to happen? • How important is it to address this issue? • What else is happening in your business? • What solution do you envision? • How will you measure success? • (What is the pain and where does it hurt?)
Resources and Constraints	• What resources will you commit to resolving the issue? • Do you have a budget range in mind? • What is your deadline? • What else is important to know? • (What constraints do you have?)

robust your assessment, the better your diagnosis will be. As your potential clients open up about their goals, and what they perceive to be the issue, pay attention to learn as much as possible and decide whether you'll need to run additional "tests" to assess the situation.

Qualify Your Prospect

In addition to understanding the problem, you have to assess whether you and your prospect can, and want to, solve it. Are they serious about finding a solution? Are they showing enough urgency or means to move forward? Are you able and interested to address the need? Before diving into these questions, get a sense for whether they are committed to a specific course of action and what they've done so far. If they are set on a specific way to resolve the issue, you'll want to know this upfront since it may or may not be beneficial to you, depending on how your services match up. For example, if you were an investment banker, and your prospect has their heart set on going public via a direct listing, the sooner you know this the better.

When a prospect has already done a fair amount of research and believes they have a clear solution to their problem, they may just want you to execute their solution and be less open to your suggestions. When possible, it's best to engage your prospect as early as possible in their decision-making process so you can help assess their situation and co-develop a solution with them. That's why the consistent follow-up with your Ideal Connections when there is no opportunity is so important (as described in Chapter 6).

If they previously engaged an external resource or tried resolving this issue internally, ask what worked and what didn't. This information can help you as you assess the situation and consider potential solutions. If you think it's unlikely that the prospect will hire you or that you can achieve the outcome they want, you might be better off ending the conversation here to not waste your prospect's time.

Urgency   When the need is urgent, and you're a good fit to help meet that need, you have a better chance of winning the business quickly. You want to know if your prospect is coming to you for a "painkiller" or a "vitamin." People often forget to take their vitamins, but rarely forget their painkillers. When they're in pain, they want relief as soon as possible, raising the urgency. When their need is urgent, your prospect will typically be less price sensitive as well. Say you're a regulatory compliance consultant and you're being vetted to advise a client. The client will likely have less urgency around engaging you to help with a typical audit than when they've already been notified by the SEC, FDA, IRS, or other agency that an action has been commenced. To gauge your prospect's urgency, try asking the following questions:

- "On a scale from 1 to 10, how important is it for you to solve the problem?"
- "What happens if you don't solve it?"
- "How will you be better off if you achieve your goal?"

These questions will help uncover what they stand to gain if they resolve the issue, and more importantly, what they might lose if they *don't* resolve it. The response to these questions will give you a sense of how motivated they might be to make a real change to improve their situation. The higher the priority, the more commitment there will be to address it.

Budget Although most prospects will hesitate to reveal their budget, they should have a clear sense for where the budget will come from and be willing to share that information. If you sense there really isn't any budget allocated to resolve this issue, then it's probably not a major problem for the firm. If that's the case, then they're likely still in research mode and may take much longer to decide whether they'll hire you, or anyone else for that matter. Ask them some form of the following to gain insight on whether or not their budget is realistic (and if they can afford you):

- "How do you typically fund these initiatives?"
- "Have you thought about the investment appropriate to resolve this issue?"

- "Where will the budget come from to resolve this issue?"
- "What's your budget range?"

These questions may also help you find the true decision maker since the budget often resides with that person. Depending on your prospects' experience buying your service, they may look to you to guide them on what the budget should be. The size of the budget will also affect how you win the work. A contract that is in the eight-figure range will be treated differently than a contract in the five-figure range. The bigger the budget, the more stakeholders will be involved in the vetting process. That means you'll need to build relationships with every group involved and potentially navigate the company's internal political landscape.

Decision-Making Process, Timeline, and Metrics for Success
Understanding the prospects' decision-making process and timeline is crucial for a number of reasons. If your main contact doesn't, or can't, provide a clear timeline or process, you're likely not dealing with the decision-maker. Alternatively, your contact may not have internal support for this initiative yet and is just browsing for ideas on how to solve their problem. Most people who are serious about looking for a solution will have a clear sense for timing and how they will measure success. Consider posing the following questions:

- "What is the decision-making process and timeline, and where are you in the process?"
- "How will you assess performance?"
- "How will addressing this need impact your key performance indicators?"

- "What are the most important criteria for this decision?"
- "If hired, who will my team and I be working with most closely?"

The more clearly you understand how your prospects will measure success, the easier it'll be for you to show your impact and keep your promise of value. Further, these questions will likely reveal whether you're in a competitive situation, and who the other stakeholders might be who can influence the decision. When you know the decision-making process, you'll have a better sense for how best to drive the process forward.

Practical Tip

In your first meeting with prospects, unless they ask you, "What do you think?" stick with *asking questions*, not *providing a solution*. You can always send a potential solution as a follow-up.

"How Much Will This Cost?"

Sometimes your prospect will bring up price during the assessment stage to get a sense for what it might cost to solve their problem (more on negotiating price in Chapter 11). They may be asking because they have not engaged an external resource for this need before and genuinely don't know the cost range for your type of services. They might also just be shopping around for the lowest price. Make a mental note of when your prospect asks about pricing. If they ask upfront, they may view your service as a commodity, thinking there could be an off-the-shelf solution. It could also indicate that they are limited in their budget authority and doing research for the actual decision maker.

Either way, it means the person asking may not appreciate your differentiators. It doesn't mean you should give up pursuing the business; it just means you'll have to approach the conversation differently.

As a rule of thumb, it's best to discuss fees only after you have a good sense of the problem and the potential solution. Sharing pricing too early in the process creates a few risks. First, you may price yourself out, especially if you and your prospect are not fully on the same page on the issue to be solved and the way to solve it. Or you may undersell yourself and quote a price you regret. Without being clear on the issue, there's a real possibility that your quote doesn't fit the actual scope of the engagement. One way to address premature pricing questions is to share the different factors that impact pricing, highlighting a few you don't have the answer to yet.

For example, you might say, "The pricing depends on the number of specialists staffed on the engagement along with the timing for the deliverable. I'll be happy to share concrete pricing once we pin down those factors. Do you have a budget range in mind? If so, that can help us narrow potential solutions that fit your budget while still achieving your outcome." This can especially be helpful with bigger projects, where pricing is less certain so early on.

If asked to send pricing by email, offer to discuss live so you can gauge their reaction in real-time. If they insist, you might offer a range of prices. By giving a range, you can address the question without limiting yourself or pricing yourself out of the opportunity. If they can't meet your lowest price point, then you may want to disengage anyway. Try saying, "Based on what we've discussed so far, the pricing will likely range from $28,000 to $135,000 depending on the options you choose. This may change as we learn more. How does that fit with what you've budgeted?"

Or if you have flexibility around pricing, one way to keep the conversation going is to say, "There are certainly providers who charge less and some who charge more. It depends on the level of service you're seeking and the scope of the deliverable. I am confident that if it's something that you believe is worth resolving, then we can find a way forward."

Step 2: Diagnose

After the assessment is complete, your prospects will be awaiting your diagnosis. Before you share your thoughts, though, ask if there is anyone else who should be a part of this conversation. This question can help ensure the right people are involved in the discussion. Ideally, you'll want the key decision makers and stakeholders present so they can directly hear your assessment. There's nothing worse than meticulously sharing a diagnosis that gets passed up the chain of command only for it to get lost in translation by the time it reaches the decision maker. By providing your diagnosis directly to the leaders calling the shots, you can gauge their reactions, clarify your points, and immediately address any of their questions, objections, or feedback.

Keep in mind that depending on your prospect's buying process, meeting with all the key decision-makers may not be possible. Regardless, once you have a good sense of the issue, you'll confirm your understanding of the situation and share your prognosis of what will happen if the issue is not addressed. If done right, your prospect should feel confident that you fully understand what's going on and have experience solving it. More importantly, your prospect should see the value of solving the issue and express their commitment to address it.

Confirm Your Understanding

When you explain your diagnosis, you need to show your prospects you've listened to them, understand their situation, and firmly grasp what they're trying to do. In a workshop my colleagues and I went through with ex-FBI negotiator Chris Voss, he shared a practical way to know whether people you're speaking to feel as if they've been heard. The phrase to listen for after you playback the issue is "That's right," as opposed to "You're right." When the other person says, "You're right," they are appeasing your ego and have likely not bought into your reflection of the situation. When you hear a "That's right," the other person is acknowledging the issue directly and showing you they agree with your interpretation. Make sure to reiterate the problem back to them in a way that reflects what they've shared with you, then listen for a "That's right."

For example, a COO for a top investment management firm was considering Exec|Comm to work with a team of their senior portfolio managers. She started describing some of the core issues she was hearing from her business development team around the portfolio managers' ability to read the room and engage their clients. As I summarized what I had heard during her explanation, she replied, "That's right. That's exactly the issue." Once she recognized that I understood the problem, I felt comfortable bringing up a few more symptoms she *hadn't* mentioned, but that I thought she was likely experiencing. I added, "They are probably sharing too many details about their investment approach and not tying it to the immediate needs of the client or really engaging the client in a meaningful way."

The COO responded, "Exactly," and went on to share, "We recently lost a piece of business to a competitor because the client just didn't connect with the portfolio manager. How do you typically coach someone who has this issue?" Because I was able to articulate her pain points and show that I had dealt with similar challenges in the past, she was even more confident in my diagnosis and ability to solve her problem.

Share the Prognosis

Once you've confirmed your understanding of the problem, and the potential root cause, paint a clear picture of what the outcomes might look like when the issue is addressed. To help raise the importance of resolving this problem, show how the outcome advances their firm's key strategy. As mentioned, you also want to highlight what happens if they don't resolve the issue. In your prognosis, describe what will happen to the key metrics if they keep the status quo and the current issue persists. If they did not share key metrics, highlight the impact on their profits. For example, will revenue go down or costs go up if the issue doesn't get resolved? Point out how doing nothing may lead to:

- Flattening revenues
- Low growth
- Costly customer acquisition
- Poor employee or client retention and satisfaction
- Wasted time and low productivity
- Low return on invested capital
- Weak reputation

When sharing your prognosis, although you want to raise the priority-level, you don't want to rush your prospects. If it sounds like you're cajoling them to do something, they may begin to wonder whether you're acting in their best interest or yours. Instead, present your prognosis in a matter-of-fact manner, and ask for their thoughts. When they reach their own conclusion that something needs to be done, they're more likely to buy into solving it. And if the implications of resolving the issue are compelling, your prospect will feel a sense of urgency to act now.

Step 3: Prescribe

Once your prospect is confident about your diagnosis and open to taking action, you can share your potential solution, which will include what the experience will be like, how much it will cost, and any follow-up solutions or foreseeable complications. Then you need to manage the prospects' reaction. If they say "yes," it is time to move forward with the plan. If it's out of their budget, then you'll want to help them think through whether the missed opportunity or growing issue is worth expanding the budget. They may still decide after exploring different options that the problem is not worth fixing for the money, time, and people needed to support the project.

Before you prescribe your solution, build space to hear from your prospect. You might use language like, "I have some ideas, but let me know what you're thinking so far," or "Before I share my thoughts, what questions do you have or what else should I know?" This space allows them to explain where they are based on what they've heard, which may impact what you recommend and how you present it.

Propose the Solution

When prescribing a solution, tie it back to the desired result your prospect is excited about reaching, or the bleak future they're hoping to avoid. Highlight the benefits they will gain from working with you using the universal motivators of time, feelings, and money. Whenever you can help them save time or use it more effectively; feel good by reducing risk and stress, enhancing reputation, status, or power; or make or save money, they will be more likely to proceed.

Although most people will position their solution as leading to a gain, you might more effectively get your prospect's buy-in by framing your solution as preventing a loss. Research shows that the pain of losing is psychologically twice as powerful as the pleasure of gaining.[2] When you highlight the pain, people are more likely to respond. For example, contrast "I recommend this approach since it'll help you reduce client attrition" (preventing loss), versus "I recommend this approach since it'll help you retain more clients" (keeping gains). Think about a typical solution you might present, and see if you can highlight the pain it'll relieve.

Your solution should not seem like a silver bullet. It's likely your prospect's problem is complex—if it was simple, they would have already solved it. Acknowledging the nuances of the situation will help improve your prospect's confidence that you understand the flexibility needed to address the problem. When you're ready to present your solution, consider language like, "Because you're [context and problem], we recommend [solution] to [prevent loss or attain gain]." For example, "Because you're in a competitive industry, and you're losing clients quickly, we recommend you merge with Company XYZ to prevent a cash crunch from impacting your operations."

After explaining the details of your solution, gain consensus on the key deliverables and metrics for success. You'll want to have a clear sense for what you're promising if they decide to hire you. Once you feel you and your prospect are on the same page, it's time to move on to the final step.

Close the Deal

If your prospect hires you, all your work has paid off. If your prospect goes with someone else or decides not to fix the problem, it might be considered a loss . . . this time. It doesn't mean there wasn't value gained for your firm or you. If you handled the process well, then even if you didn't win the business, you deepened a relationship, and the next time you connect with that client, you're connecting as a known entity. View your efforts as the "tuition" paid for the worthwhile learning experience and connections you've made in the process. Although the lessons you learn throughout these steps are valuable in and of themselves, revenue is still the name of the game. To maximize your chances of being hired, you need to become skilled at the three critical components to the close: timing, positioning, and delivery.

Timing   No one likes to feel pressured into buying something—it doesn't matter if it's a big purchase item like a home or something as simple as a new shirt. And this, of course, holds true when it comes to your services. If you ask prospects to buy before they're ready, their default answer will be "no." The timing of this ask is crucial; to get it right, consider the prospects' decision-making timeline and gauge their interest for a solution after hearing your ideas. If your prospect doesn't seem engaged to solve the problem, you'll need to get more buy-in before you go in for the close.

Try putting out feelers, or trial closes. These are asks that make sense only if the person intends to move forward. For example, most large firms require a Master Services Agreement between their firm and the service provider. Since this process is both time and resource intensive, firms are likely not going to explore this option unless they felt ready to move forward. A typical trial close you might use is, "Since it usually takes some time to work through the Master Services Agreement, would it make sense to connect with your procurement team to start this process in tandem as we pin down the exact solution? This way, if you decide to move forward, we can do so quickly." If they say "no," then you know they're still deliberating. If they say "yes," they're likely open to you asking for the business. Other trial closes include setting a date for a potential pilot or gaining access to an executive sponsor.

Throughout the sales process, be attuned to your prospects' timeline. People buy when they convince themselves, not when you convince them. As they listen to your assessment, diagnosis, and prescription, help them feel in control of the process. When you lay out your diagnosis and prognosis well, your prospect should feel a strong urge to solve their issue and actively ask you about their options.

If you know you are in a competitive situation and asked to participate in a bake-off or final pitch, request to be the last to present. Your prospect will then listen to your approach in light of the other presentations. Their questions to you will likely reveal the key criteria they're using to decide between you and your competitors. They may bring up the ideas they liked from the other presentations and see if you can do something similar. By going last, you also take advantage of the "recency effect," the bias that ideas that are explained last in a group of ideas are remembered more clearly, making you and your solution more memorable. If you're not the last team to present because of scheduling reasons, ask your prospect if you can come back to address any follow-up questions after the last team. Although it may be unlikely to be brought back without bringing the other teams back as well, it doesn't hurt to ask.

Positioning   Once you decide it's the right time to close, you'll want to be thoughtful in how you frame the ask. One of your goals is to instill confidence that you can reliably solve the problem. The key words here are *you* and *reliably*. Your prospects will want to show the rest of the organization they're making a good decision by bringing you on. In addition to expending the firm's time, effort, and money, your prospects shoulder the risk of hiring you (and the blame if your solution fails). When it comes to closing a deal then, you want to remove as much risk as possible for your prospect.

Understanding this perspective, focus on positioning yourself as the most *reliable* candidate. You can show how well you've executed this solution before. Your client list can serve as a proxy for your quality. If you've already been vetted by other prestigious organizations, you not only benefit from social proof, but you also reduce the prospect's risk of hiring you. You can share client testimonials, case studies, or your track record, including quantifiable results you were able to achieve. For example, you might highlight a five-times return on investment, a two-day reduction in lead times, or a 35 percent increase in revenue. (One caveat is showing ROI that seems too good to be true; outsized rewards translate into a perception of outsized risk, which can derail a deal.) When you present these stats, you reassure your prospect by sharing a clear vision of what they will receive if they hire you.

When prospects are stringently vetting you and asking about your methodology and other details, they're seeking assurance that your approach will actually lead to the results discussed. Hear these questions not as threats or challenges, but as deep interest in moving the process forward with you. They are doing their due diligence. Hearing their questions in the most positive light possible will enable you to respond most openly. This is not the time to impress them with the theoretical basis for your approach or to tell them about some new, but unproven technology you think might work. Put them at ease by showing your methodology is tried and true and explain your approach in a logical and easy-to-understand manner. If your approach is a visible one like communication skills training, you might offer a showcase. If it's a technology solution, you can offer a demo or trial period. You can also reduce your prospects' risk by making your fee contingent on results or some other guarantee of satisfaction.

No matter how long you've been in the business, there will always be someone else out there with more experience, bigger accolades, or higher-profile clients. Don't focus on your competition. Focus on your prospects. My team and I were once being considered alongside another company whose staff included a Nobel Laureate. While we have some very talented people on our team, none of us have been honored in Stockholm, yet. So, instead of focusing on what we didn't have, we turned the focus back on the client and asked them what outcomes they were looking to achieve. Once it sounded like their needs aligned with what we had to offer, we focused on what we could do, and not what we don't or couldn't do. We acknowledged the gap upfront and highlighted the relevance of our experience: "We don't have Nobel Laureates on our team, but we do have experienced coaches with backgrounds similar to your leaders. Many of our coaches have not only helped other executives tackle the challenges you've shared, but they've overcome similar ones in their own careers, better equipping them to help others do the same." Ultimately, the client saw the value in both firms and decided to hire both of us as part of their pool of executive coaches.

Remember, no one's perfect, so don't pretend to be. If you are aware of any gaps in the services you're offering, be transparent and upfront about them. Though you may feel uncomfortable about raising perceived shortcomings, leading with them has been shown to actually disarm prospects.[3] When you call out your flaws, you make it harder for prospects to come up with additional weaknesses about your services. You also appear more trustworthy since others expect you to stick only to the positives when pitching your services. Of course, you'll still need to show you're competent at solving the issue.

No matter how you position yourself, tailor what you're saying to your prospects by mirroring the language they've been using throughout your interactions. By playing back the key points, along with your solution, using their own words, you increase the chances of your recommendation resonating. When meeting with your prospects, jot down verbatim any key phrases you're hearing that you may use later in your proposal. If you get the positioning right, the other person should feel like your solution is exactly what they were looking for.

Delivery After you've figured out the best timing and positioning, then you'll want to think how you will deliver the close. As the rainmaker, you will likely be making the ask, but depending on the situation and cultural nuances, you may decide a more senior colleague might be the better messenger. Some cultures prefer a direct approach, while others prefer back channeling. For direct cultures, you might say, "You mentioned wanting to get started in the summer, what adjustments to our plan would help us deliver the best solution for you?" More indirect asks might go through a third-party advisor or use language like, "Did you get a chance to review the proposal?"

Make the ask in a calm, matter-of-fact manner. If you show discomfort or hesitation, you will put the prospects on guard. Do not be overly deferential, either, unless the specific culture you're working within requires it. Remember, even though they are the ones paying your fee, the relationship is a business transaction—you are providing value, not extracting value from them. Don't treat it as if they are doing you a favor by hiring you.

As decision-making is becoming more decentralized, especially for large engagements, you will need to know where you stand with multiple stakeholders—budget owner, project leader, execution team, procurement, and other related parties. They each have their own needs and goals, and if they have a say in the decision, you'll need to make sure they're on your side.

Sometimes people offer to send a proposal to their clients as a way to move the process forward or close the deal. Don't offer to do so, however, until the prospect has asked you for one and after it is clear what they want you to send. If you haven't agreed on an overall approach, you'll find yourself spending too much time considering different scenarios and guessing at what your prospects want to see.

In some cases, you might be asked to complete a more formal request for proposal (RFP). An RFP may be required for the prospects' vendor management process, but make sure it is worth your effort. RFPs can be time consuming and often put the pressure on you to negotiate with yourself. If you receive an RFP from a prospect you've never been in touch with before, or if you haven't already gone through the assess-diagnose-prescribe steps, it's possible that you're not a serious contender for the project. The RFP format is designed to commoditize your service. The way the questions are laid out, it is hard to show how your solution differentiates, and it could be used as a way to increase competition between vendors or bubble up ideas for execution in-house. If you decide to pursue RFPs, track your success rate in winning the RFPs you submit and the time spent in filling them out. This data will help you decide whether it's worth the resources you're expending to continue pursuing them in the future.

When sending a proposal, confirm the elements the prospects want to see. Though typically they'll just be looking for a concise articulation of the problem, your approach, a statement of work, and your pricing, terms, and conditions, they may ask for something more tailored. No matter what you include, remember the proposal confirms what you and your prospect have agreed to—it is not an effective medium on its own for pitching your services.

Manage the Response

The most important part of the close is to *ask for the business*. Doctors "close" their patients every day. Typically, they ask, "So, what would you like to do?" or "Would you like to move forward with the recommended approach?" You'll get a few possible responses, the best, of course, being "yes." If they say "no," don't act disappointed. Consider how doctors respond. They stay detached and avoid getting emotionally invested in their patients' decisions. After they share their recommended treatment, they are not devastated if their patients decide to go for a second opinion or to decline the treatment. They also don't try to push their treatment on their patients. Doctors understand their role is to help patients do what they already want to do. If the patient is not comfortable with the doctor's recommendation, the doctor doesn't take the patient's decision personally. It was just the patient's choice. So, when your prospect moves in a different direction, don't challenge them. Acknowledge there are many ways for the prospect to achieve their goals and express your willingness to be a sounding board and resource in the future.

You're building your reputation, so you'll want to handle rejection graciously, or else you won't be invited to pitch for other business. Use this setback as an opportunity to learn—maybe your solution was not a good fit, or you failed to present your solution effectively. Maybe your proposal did not accurately represent what you are able to do. Maybe a key influencer was backing a competitor's bid. Ask for feedback on what you can continue to develop to be better poised for future opportunities. Remember that you won't win them all, and you are better off with a definitive "no" than an everlasting "maybe."

The third possibility is that they'll just say they are "not sure." This may be the most frustrating of responses, but it also opens a whole new conversation that can push that "maybe" to a "yes." As shown in the tactics in Chapter 11, when you come to this point, you'll want to address your prospects' objections, hesitations, or concerns.

The way you conduct yourself will give prospects insight into what it would be like working with you. All of these interactions throughout the three-step process and closing are like a drawn-out audition. Since that's the case, look for ways to make every interaction worthwhile and give a sneak peek into how you operate. Some people may want you to be supportive, and others expect you to challenge them. Most will want you to be responsive, flexible, and focused on them. As you interact together, show them you have their best interest in mind. Highlight the risks of their doing nothing and demonstrate how you can reliably help them reach their goals. If you treat the prospect right throughout this process, the close might be as simple as asking, "What do you think? Would you like to work together?"

Metrics

The following metrics should help you assess how well you're executing the three-step Assess, Diagnose, Prescribe process to close a concrete opportunity. As with the metrics in Chapter 6, decide which ones work best for you, and when possible, automate your calculation of these metrics.

Metric	How to calculate	Implications/Application
Close Rate	$\dfrac{\text{\# of opportunities won}}{\text{\# of opportunities considered}}$	Shows you how many opportunities you've been considered for and how many you actually win. The higher the close rate, the better you are at qualifying and closing deals. In addition to tracking this metric, keep a list of reasons you won or lost a deal to better fine tune how you can increase your close rate.

Metric	How to calculate	Implications/Application
Average Sales Cycle	Average time between notice of concrete opportunities to actual date of closing the deal.	The length of your sales cycle depends on your service, your client's buying process, and the timing of their outreach to you. Your goal is to shorten the length it takes to make a sale by building stronger relationships, raising urgency, and asking for the close. When you have a sense for the average sales cycle, you can also gauge when you need to be more patient, and when you can likely drive the process forward.
Win/Loss ratio by step (Assess, Diagnose, Prescribe)	Count # of opportunities lost during the Assess, Diagnose, and Prescribe steps over the course of a year.	Allows you to glean insights by tracking when you typically fall out of the sales cycle, especially when prospects do not give you a reason on why they decided to go with another solution provider.
Sales Efficiency	$\dfrac{\text{Revenue}}{\text{\# of sales interactions}}$	Provides a sense for how efficient you are with your sales activity. The higher the ratio, the more revenue you're closing per sales interaction.
Average Opportunity Size	$\dfrac{\text{Total Revenue}}{\text{Total \# of opportunities}}$ (You can use total # of opportunities considered or closed.)	Look for ways to increase the size of each opportunity to improve this metric. When you qualify prospects, consider becoming more selective over time, turning down smaller opportunities.
Sales Cost Ratio	$\dfrac{\text{Annual sales expenses}}{\text{Annual revenue generated}}$	Sales expenses include commission, 3rd party fees, travel, marketing, support-staff involvement, and any other related costs to your sales activities. If you are measured on your profitability within your firm, minimize your costs of selling if your ratio is high.

CHAPTER

8

Success Upon Success: When You're Uncovering Additional Needs

Chapter 8: Success Upon Success: When You're Uncovering Additional Needs

Once you've been engaged by a client, your business development efforts don't stop there. Chul Pak, Anti-Trust Partner at the law firm Wilson Sonsini, reminds us that, "at this point, doing the work is stressful and it consumes a lot of time, of course, but you need to at least devote a certain amount of time to what you might call critical business development." Pak continues, "I'm always thinking about the pipeline, as a partner in particular, because it's one thing to do the work, but you've got to think about what the revenue stream is going to look like two, three, or even four years out." Though you're regularly pulled away to deliver on the work you've sold, you still need to carve out time to continue building your book of business.

For those who are just shifting from doing the work to selling the work, Pak suggests focusing on existing clients. He notes that for associates in a law firm, "the likelihood of generating new business outside on your own, particularly at a big law firm, is extremely slim." Every interaction with an existing client provides an opportunity to uncover other needs you may be able to address. Since you'll be spending a lot of your time with your clients while you're delivering the work, existing client engagements offer numerous chances to help you fill your pipeline. If you serve your current clients well, they will invite you back and consistently tell others about you.

Growing your business with existing clients not only increases your revenue and visibility, it also enhances your expertise. By helping your clients meet their evolving needs, your practical expertise grows, and your value to your clients continues to increase. As you meet more of your clients' needs, they'll increase their commitment to you. To kick off this mutually beneficial relationship, you'll want to follow a clear strategy to keep your clients happy and increase the business you do together.

Embed, Expand, and Establish

During an active client engagement, find additional opportunities by progressing through the three-step Embed, Expand, Establish process, as shown in Figure 8.1.

With any engagement, especially your first one with a new client, your goal is to stabilize your position and embed yourself so your new client sees tremendous value in working with you. Once you're embedded, you'll be better positioned to look for expansion opportunities by up-selling, cross-selling, and asking for referrals. As you land additional opportunities with your client, you'll continue to embed and expand until you fully establish yourself as the go-to provider of your type of services. Most large corporations use more than one law firm, accounting firm, and investment bank, depending on the nature of their business. You may not be able to keep the competition out, but you can increase your chances of getting the lion's share of the work the more comprehensively you service the client.

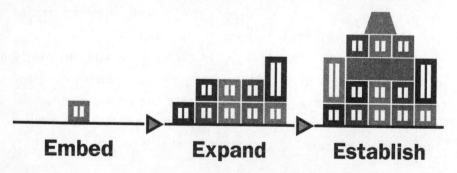

FIGURE 8.1 Three-Step Embed, Expand, Establish Process

When you become adept at employing this three-step process, you can use it to extend beyond just one client, embedding, extending, and establishing yourself across an entire industry. After you're embedded with one client, you build up transferable expertise and knowledge valuable to other clients. From there, you can expand to other organizations by a referral, reaching out directly with your enhanced credibility, or reconnecting with one of your buyers who moved to another organization. As you work with different companies within an industry, you'll build up both industry knowledge and expertise to establish yourself in this sector.

Embed

The first time a client hires you, it's normally because of the relationship you've built with them and their faith in your ability to deliver. The next and each subsequent time they hire you will depend on the quality of your most recent engagement and how well you kept the promises you made to them. Acquiring new clients usually takes more time, energy, and money than retaining existing ones because you need to build a trusting relationship where one doesn't currently exist. It's difficult to develop a substantive book of business if your clients constantly leave you, and you have to rebuild your business up from the ground floor every year. During the sales process, your clients valued their experience with you enough to engage you. Now that you're hired, it's time to elevate their experience so they keep bringing you back. You must fully understand your clients and their needs, becoming so close to their issues you are difficult to replace. There are three surefire ways to embed yourself in this way: Consistently demonstrate reliability, remain responsive, and deepen your relationships.

Reliability

After you win a project, get started immediately. Though you sufficiently demonstrated your *potential* to add value while they were a prospect, you now want your new client to *experience* that value. The longer you wait to begin, the more likely they will question their decision to hire you. Put their mind at ease by reaching out to them with a clear execution game plan and next steps. By showing that you're ready to get to work right away, you'll help them feel good about their decision to hire you. This punctuality also signals that your attentiveness is the way you operate, not just a façade you put on to win their business.

Your clients will expect you to follow through on your commitments and treat their people with respect. But meeting these expectations will only create a complaint-free situation, the lowest bar possible in client service—this will not create the kind of relationship you need to actually grow your business. To embed yourself, you'll need to go above and beyond. That means actively showing your clients that you're on it and proving to them quickly that they don't need to worry about you, especially when you engage with their senior stakeholders. Keep them well informed of the engagement's status and help them solve challenges as they arise. If you spot an issue or potential risk, warn them as soon as possible so they can get in front of it and not be blindsided. You want them to feel confident that you have everything under control.

That said, be attuned to how much your clients want to be involved. Then interact with them in the way they find most helpful. Some may want detailed weekly updates and daily check-ins throughout the engagement. Others would rather remain as hands-off as possible and not hear from you unless an issue arises. The more your clients can rely on you to take care of what needs to be done, the more they will feel comfortable partnering with you.

Throughout the engagement, stay focused on your clients and find ways to make their lives easier. You might notice tasks that you can easily take off their plate, or small details you can help your clients manage so they don't need to worry about them. For example, you might offer to automate a manual process for a client or build a summary dashboard they can use to track the engagement status in real-time. You want clients to miss you if you were gone. Actively catch problems they may have overlooked and note anything you see or hear that may be of interest to them. They should know you have their back and that you not only show up consistently, but you're always looking out for them.

Responsiveness

Being dependable is great, but to create an elevated experience, you also need to be accessible. When your clients contact you, they typically want to tell you something at that moment—that's why they are calling, emailing, or texting you in the first place. They may not expect you to be "on call" or deliver what they need without delay, but they will want to know you at least received their message. If you respond to their questions or requests quickly and consistently, you show them they're your priority. The longer you make them wait, however, the less important they will feel. If your clients start to think they're not a priority, especially when they have an emergency, they may start looking for other resources who may be more accessible.

You may hear advice to the contrary, like "You shouldn't respond too quickly. It makes you seem overeager. Don't make yourself look so available." The logic goes that if you respond too quickly, you will seem as if you're not busy enough, implying either you're not working hard for your clients or you're not in high demand (both of which might give your clients second thoughts on working with you in the first place). It's also possible that you'll set an expectation you feel you can't live up to, feeling pressure to *always* respond quickly, even when it may be difficult or impossible to do so. Though there is some truth to this guidance, it's focused more on *your* needs than your clients'.

When anyone makes a request, they prefer to get a response as fast as possible. In addition, we have all gotten used to shorter wait times—same-day shipping, high-speed internet, text messaging. Remember when it took a day to download a movie, or when Netflix would send you physical DVDs you'd have to return via mail? Our expectations have changed. Just like you don't appreciate being made to wait nowadays, your clients don't, either.

If you are truly too busy to respond in a timely fashion on a regular basis, you may want to hire an assistant or a client service professional who can reply on your behalf. Working 24/7 is not the goal here—the goal is putting a system in place that gives your clients an extraordinary experience. If your client has ever followed up with you on a previous request, that's a sure sign you're not responsive enough. As you become more successful, your responsiveness will carry that much more weight. Many C-suite executives aim to respond within 12 hours of getting an email, despite all of their responsibilities. Your clients should feel like they are your number-one client, and that you're willing to go out of your way to support them.

The ultimate form of responsiveness is anticipating someone's needs—responding *before* they even ask, or meeting needs they didn't realize they had or hadn't articulated yet. The more time you spend with your clients, the more chances you'll have to understand their preferences and goals, personal and professional. During your conversations, keep your antennas alert for these signals and reflect on what you hear to anticipate their needs. Based on where you are in the engagement, ask yourself, "What might they expect from me at this point?" Deliver on that expectation before they ask.

For example, you might learn this is the first time your buyer is owning an engagement of this magnitude, and they want to show their senior executives they can take on other major responsibilities. In addition to making this engagement a resounding success, try sharing best practices with your buyer around strategic stakeholder management and effective ways to showcase their work to their senior stakeholders. You might go a step further and help them prepare content for when they update their executives, not only saving them time, but also ensuring they're hitting the main points that are important to highlight. By being attuned to your clients' unstated goals, you can find ways to pleasantly surprise them, responding to "unasked asks."

Relationships

Once you've been hired, you'll find your clients are more open to sharing information with you since you're now on the same team, working side by side. Instead of using a critical lens to vet you, they will now look to partner with you to achieve the agreed-upon outcomes. This partnership may lead to a better understanding of your clients' organizational needs and personal aspirations. This privileged information, along with access to decisions makers, can help you discover ways to add more value to your clients. Chul Pak, from Wilson Sonsini, says close relationships with decision makers develop when those clients are comfortable with you, and when they experience a sense of trust and confidence. "I think those are the distinguishing factors as to why certain clients stay with me and others don't," Pak admits. The better your relationships, the bigger the commitment you can make with each other, and the further you embed yourself.

Although you might want to reassure your clients they've made a good decision of hiring you by showing off your value, resist putting the focus on you—keep the focus on them. When possible, instead of holding court and telling your clients all the things they need to fix, look for ways to help them "trip over the truth." According to *New York Times* bestselling authors Chip and Dan Heath, you want to create situations where your clients immediately realize a powerful insight on their own that changes the way they see their business.[1] When they recognize this insight for themselves, they will more likely commit to taking action, making them more open to your ideas and increasing your chances of success.

The Heaths recount how Microsoft executive Scott Guthrie was tasked with rolling out Microsoft's cloud platform Azure. As part of his process, Scott interviewed customers and learned that though they found Azure to be good, they also found it difficult to use. Instead of just telling his team to fix the issue, Scott asked them to develop an app using the Azure platform. As his team struggled with what should have been a straightforward task, they realized for themselves the serious problems their users had been experiencing. When you help your clients see the breakthrough on their own, you show you have their best interests at heart and that your focus is on their success, not necessarily your hand in it.

Another way to show how invested you are in your clients' success is to make your main buyers at the client look and feel good. When they feel recognized by others in their firm or their reputation is enhanced because of you, they're more likely to want to keep working with you. Pak emphasizes, "Showing recognition of the value of that person in front of their management goes a long way. Make that person look good so that they get that bonus or land that promotion. If you help them succeed, that person will want to hire you again." In fact, Pak has even been told by his buyers that they appreciate how he makes them shine in front of their bosses. As you think about your current client engagements, look for a chance to put in a good word and play up your buyer's value to their key stakeholders, giving them the credit for the progress you're making together.

When your buyers gain positive visibility because of you, they'll feel great about the relationship and even more pleased with having hired you. Not only are you getting the job done, you're helping to advance their career. Further, as you receive positive feedback from your buyers' different stakeholders, ask them to share their experience with your buyer. For example, if the treasurer enjoys working with you and your team, you might ask them to share their positive feedback with the CFO, your main buyer. This way your buyer receives confirmation from their colleagues that hiring you was a great choice, and again, they receive credit for the good work you're doing.

In some situations, your relationship with your clients may develop into a genuine friendship. But just as you may click with certain people and not others, not every client will become a friend. If you feel comfortable developing the relationship in this deeper way, you'll likely find yourself showing up for your clients on a more personal level. You may be invited to weddings, bar mitzvahs, and many of life's other milestones. Perhaps you will guide them through a career transition, or help their kids find an internship. Or maybe you just grab lunch with them once in a while to catch up.

With all friendships, or any relationship for that matter, remember you need to be genuine. Pretending to be someone's friend to develop business will not end well. Also, this "friendship approach" may not suit you, and that's okay, too. Whether you consider each other "friends" or not, a strong professional relationship, in which your clients can count on you to get the job done well, will ensure they want to keep working with you.

Leave your buyers with an experience where instead of saying, "Thank you for coming," they ask, "When are you coming back?"

Expand

Once you're embedded with your clients and they feel fully confident about your ability to deliver results, you're on fertile ground to discover additional opportunities. It's generally easier to sell to clients who've already bought from you and are happy with their choice. When your clients value their partnership with you, they may be more open to exploring how else you might work together, or willing to recommend you to others. The three main ways to expand on your current engagement are to up-sell, by upgrading the current service to your client, cross-sell, by supporting your current service with additional services, and be referred to other buyers.

Uncover Opportunities to Up-Sell or Cross-Sell

Up-selling and cross-selling expand your business with an existing client by meeting their other pressing needs. When you're delivering work, it's easy to focus only on the task at hand, but you'll want to keep an ear open for other needs. These may come up as you interact with different teams, during a touch-base meeting with your buyer, or in a conversation with key stakeholders. When you find out about an acute need you can help with, you might offer a premium add-on (up-sell) or additional services from your firm (cross-sell). For example, imagine your client engages you to help with their tax filing. During the engagement, you hear they would prefer to fast track this engagement to free up resources for their current global expansion. You might offer to add resources on your end to help move up the timeline (up-sell) while also offering to introduce your client to your cross-border transactions team (cross-sell).

Sometimes, if it's your first engagement with a client, they may hire you for a specific service and remain unaware of your other capabilities. As mentioned in Chapter 6, look for ways to educate them about the breadth of your services to be considered for additional needs. For example, when you're casually catching up, find natural points in the conversation to mention work you were just delivering for another client. Or you can flat out ask, "Would you be interested in learning about new ideas we see gaining traction at other firms in your industry?"

If you've been working with a client for a while, and especially if they are a large organization, share the work you're doing in one area with your Ideal Connections in other areas. At big companies, different teams may not have the chance to connect with each other on a regular basis and may benefit from having you as the conduit for sharing knowledge. If you work for an organization with multiple practices, broaden your knowledge of these other services so you can better cross-sell your colleagues' capabilities in these conversations as well.

Staying attuned to your clients' pressing needs can direct how you develop your own capabilities. As you learn about your client's new challenges, you may decide to enhance your own capabilities so you can step up to continue supporting them. For example, if your client is grappling with the tax implications of buying and selling digital currencies and assets, you may invest time and energy learning about the updated tax code and new regulations in this area. As you expand your services, not only can you better add value to your existing client base, but you also widen your prospecting pool. The more needs you can meet, the more chances you have to expand your business.

Get Referred

Referrals are one of the best ways to land new opportunities. Clients refer you when they hear from a colleague about a specific need. Because the client's referral is an implicit endorsement of you and the quality of your services, you launch to the head of the pack if the new potential buyer is considering multiple service providers. Often, the referring client will share the positive experience they've had with you, further bolstering your credibility, and potentially putting you on the fast track to close the deal. If you're referred to your clients' colleagues within the same organization, you'll likely be seen as less risky. It will also be easier to onboard you since you already have a working relationship with the firm, along with an approved contract and rate card.

As with many aspects of rainmaking, don't wait for the referrals to "come to you." Even if you and your client have a great relationship, they may not realize how they can help you. Or if they recognize their ability to help, they may not know whether you want it from them. That is, of course, unless you ask. That's why you'll want to proactively seek out referrals. If you're not sure whether your current or past clients are comfortable referring you directly, you can start by asking for their advice on how to expand your network within their firm. Similar to asking for introductions as a way to build your relationships with your Ideal Connections (covered in Chapter 6), there are some basic ground rules on seeking out referrals.

Don't ask your client to do something they're not comfortable with; let them choose the way they want to help you and don't persist or take it personally if it's obvious they don't want to refer you. If they recognize the great work you've done, they might still hesitate to refer you because they don't feel comfortable based on their role at the firm or they are not well networked. Just make sure your ask is something they can actually give you, and again, be okay if they say no.

For the clients who seem willing to refer you, try the following language if you're looking to be referred to someone they know:

> "Hi, Sara, I'm calling to ask for a potential favor. I recently heard your firm has put out an RFP for advisory work to support your expansion to Latin America. We've recently helped another company with a similar expansion that I think might be relevant. Would you be open to connecting us with the sponsor for that RFP and sharing your experience working with us? I'm happy to draft an email with the relevant details. Also, if you don't feel comfortable, no worries, I completely understand."

For someone they might know, such as a LinkedIn connection or a colleague who may work at the same company, consider the following:

> "Hi, Sara, I'm calling to ask for a potential favor. We've recently done some work with ABC company that I think could be a good fit for XYZ department. I'm looking to connect with a Tom Xu. Do you know him?"

If they respond affirmatively, follow it up with:

> "Tom and I are currently not connected, so I was wondering if you wouldn't mind making the introduction. Based on my research, I think he might be interested in hearing about our experience helping a company similar to his expand to Latin America. Happy to share more details if that's helpful. And no worries if you don't feel comfortable introducing us—I completely understand."

If they agree to refer you, make it easy for them to do so. Just as in the earlier example, draft a referral email they can easily edit and send.

When clients refer you to an Ideal Connection, follow-up with that connection immediately. Not only does this reflect well on you and your client, but if you wait too long, the person you were referred to may forget who referred you and why. You want to be fresh in their memory. Next, thank your client for the referral. Research has found that gratitude is more effective when you emphasize what the other person did and not how you benefited.[2] For example, instead of saying, "Thank you for the referral, Sara. I'm so excited to be working with your products team at their upcoming offsite," try, "Sara, thank you for introducing us to Ji-Hoon. I know you're busy, and I appreciate you taking the time to make that connection and putting in a good word for us." Keep your clients updated on your progress and find thoughtful ways to appreciate the people who refer you. At a minimum, send a handwritten thank-you note. Recognizing your referrers' above-and-beyond investment in you will likely lead to more referrals in the future.

The best time to ask for a referral is after a successful engagement. When coming right off a great experience, your clients are confident about your abilities and feel more comfortable recommending you. To create a window to ask for referrals, offer to set up a debrief call with your client after each engagement to discuss what went well and what could have gone better. In addition to learning relevant feedback to improve your services, the conversation should highlight what you achieved. If you've overdelivered on your promise, your client should be extremely satisfied, which sets the perfect context to ask for referrals. (In addition to referrals, you might also ask your client for a testimonial to further bolster your reputation.)

There are several ways to ask for a referral during such a meeting:

- "By any chance, would your other colleagues be interested in hearing about our recent engagement? If so, should I reach out to them directly, and would you be comfortable if I use your name as a reference?"

- "I heard another group within your company might be interested in doing something similar to what we just completed together. Do you know anyone in that group, and do you have any suggestions for the best way to approach that person?"

Once your client agrees to recommend you, they've further escalated their commitment to you and have gone from a buyer to an advocate. To tap into the power of this relationship, regularly update them on your capabilities. Even if they're not able to engage you, they might have a conversation with a colleague who can, and the update will, hopefully, trigger them to refer you. Your client advocate recognizes your worth and your ability to help their colleagues. Make sure they know you are interested in becoming a broader resource to the organization. A simple, "Please keep me in mind as other needs arise—I'm working with a few groups at your company and am always glad to be an additional resource," will likely do the trick.

Practical Tip

Make a list of your clients who have been satisfied with your performance. Reconnect with one with whom you have strong rapport and ask for a referral to someone at their organization or in their network.

Establish

Once you're embedded and you expand successfully throughout the company, you have an opportunity to fully establish yourself with your client. To become established means to become the default choice. You want your clients to feel that it's easiest for them to work with you because you know each other well and you can anticipate what they want. When you're seen as a trusted insider, your clients will funnel many of their needs through you.

No matter how established you are—your competitors are out there. Chul Pak always keeps this in mind. "There are new people coming up all the time, so competition is significant." Even with his tenure and experience, he continues to work on his skills to continue establishing himself. "It's a lot of work, thinking about the business development side. And I have to tell you, I'm constantly working at it because it's still a challenge to me. There's always another level of development that I need to improve to do even better."

One effective way to establish yourself is to amass institutional knowledge about your specific client. You can build this valuable asset by keeping track of what you're learning about the organization as you embed and expand your work to different groups. Also, if you've delivered a substantial volume of work, you've likely strengthened your relationships with not only your buyers, but also their executive-level stakeholders. When you deeply understand the company, and its political undercurrent, you become more effective at getting things done while also increasing your likelihood for success on any current and future engagements with them. You also become an insider. At that point, you truly go from seller to assistant buyer (as discussed in Chapter 3).

To solidify your status as an insider, show your clients you're "in the know." Play back comments you're hearing from other insiders, use the organization's lingo and acronyms (correctly), and exhibit your understanding of the most updated strategy or news that only someone close to the organization would be privy to (without divulging any confidential information, of course). You will know you are becoming established when your client remarks, "You know our business so well." When others within the organization see you as one of them, they're more likely to trust you with additional information. They'll also be more open to your recommendations, further increasing your value to them.

My friend, Joann, has never steered me wrong on restaurant recommendations. Whenever I have a special occasion, instead of searching on Yelp, I just shoot her a text with a general location, price point, and the occasion, and in less than an hour, she texts me with three options. She's my trusted "restaurant guide." When it comes to your clients, you want to be their trusted guide, too, not for restaurants, of course, but for any related service they may need (though they might appreciate a good restaurant rec from time to time!). When they see you as a go-to advisor, they come to you first with new needs as they arise.

To gain this coveted standing, proactively leverage both your skills and professional relationships to help your clients meet their evolving needs (see Chapter 9 for specific tactics on building a valuable network). Refer them to high-quality contacts and find natural ways to mention your additional capabilities and resources so your clients are aware of your reach. By priming your clients in this way, you're teaching them that, when they have a need, it's easier for them to check in with you first before doing a search on their own or calling anyone else. In this process, you not only save your clients time and money in finding and vetting new resources, but you're also learning about their needs and how else you can help them.

You can further establish yourself with your client by increasing the number of relationships within their organization.

You've likely started doing this when you were expanding your work, but the more of your colleagues you can embed within your client, the stronger your two firms will become intertwined. Chul Pak at Wilson Sonsini confirms this strategy. "If you're a smart partner, you don't want one touchpoint with the client. You don't want just one relationship. If there are multiple points of contact, you have greater staying power with that client." He adds, "If my senior associates have good relationships with the assistant general counsel, because they worked on a matter together, then I've got relationships with four or five people at that company, instead of that one or two that I might have." Look for chances to connect different colleagues to your clients in a value-added way. By having multiple relationship touchpoints, you strengthen the bond between your client and your firm, and you also provide the client with more coverage and responsiveness.

Watch out for potential pitfalls when you become established with your client. Like any close relationship, you run the risk of taking it for granted. Treat each engagement with the same care you would your first engagement. Even when you become the default choice to help with new needs, keep showing your gratitude and enthusiasm for the work. Put in the same effort and level of service when you were embedding yourself with the client. When your clients feel well-taken care of, they'll continue thinking of you for future opportunities.

Another pitfall when you're established with a client and delivering numerous engagements for them is the increased likelihood of something going wrong. You won't always be able to prevent a mistake, but in most cases, it's your response that matters more than the error itself. There's also a silver lining here: The way you handle a mistake may improve your client relationship, establishing you further. When you misstep, there is a four-step process you can follow to help you preserve, and possibly grow, your relationship with the client:

1. **Take ownership of the mistake and apologize to your client.** Don't deflect blame, or even worse, blame the client or their team. You're looking to defuse the situation and move forward in a positive way. Don't overcomplicate your apology, either. Just be direct. For example, if you missed a deadline, be straightforward and tell your client, "I'm sorry that we missed the deadline on this deliverable." (If there is liability involved, you'll want to consult your legal team around language.)

2. **Articulate what you did or failed to do that led to the mistake and the resulting impact on your client.** You want them to recognize that you're not only sorry for the mistake, but that you fully understand what happened, why it happened, and how it impacted them. Again, straightforward language is the best, such as "I know how important staying on track means for this project, and this delay is causing delays for you in other areas. Would it be helpful if I explained what happened?"

3. **State what you're doing to fix it and to prevent it from occurring in the future.** Doing so shows what you've learned from the mistake and reassures your client that you're actively working to prevent this issue from happening again. Your goal is to reestablish your client's confidence in you and your firm. For example, start with, "We've already added two additional staff members to the team and should have this deliverable to you by tomorrow. We will keep these members in place to help get this project on track." Then share specific preventive measures you're taking.

4. **Ask your client what you can do to make them feel whole.** Most people are reasonable and understand mistakes happen. When you focus on "making them whole," you show your commitment to the relationship by offering to do what it takes to make your client feel good about continuing their partnership with you. For example, you might say, "We want to make this up to you. What can we do to make you and your stakeholders feel whole?" Sometimes, the restitution is obvious, like waiving your fee or not charging for extra time. Even then, your clients may prefer a different approach. Let them tell you what they want, so it gives you the best chance to keep the relationship intact. If their ask is unreasonable, then this might be a relationship worth forgoing.

The goal throughout this four-step process is to confirm to your client that you're there for them and not just yourself. You're willing to take ownership of their experience and find a productive way forward. But no matter how well you own the issue or apologize, the cold, hard reality is that there will be situations where the adverse impact was so great that your client has to fire you. Hopefully, those situations are extremely rare. By following this four-step process when things go wrong, you increase the likelihood of preserving the relationship and getting a second chance.

Metrics

As with the other metrics in Part II, the following will help you assess how effective you are at implementing the rainmaker strategies. Though you don't need to use these metrics all at once, or all together, you will want some way to gain insights on how well you keep your clients happy and your ability to win additional work from existing clients. Again, automate the collection of these metrics so you can just pull up a dashboard in real-time to see how you're doing.

Metric	How to calculate	Implications/Application
# of Repeat Clients	Count the total number of clients you have this year that engaged you last year as well	This metric should increase year over year if your clients value what you bring to the relationship. If you often land the first deal, but you're not tapped for subsequent or repeat business with the same clients, you should reflect on the reason. Perhaps your client mix is too heavily weighted toward small companies that buy episodically. Maybe your offering is not resonating strongly enough, or your clients are not aware of your full capabilities and thinking of you for other needs? By understanding the reason, you can decide on what to do next.
Annual Client Churn Rate (full year)	$\dfrac{\text{\# of clients last year who didn't buy from you this year}}{\text{Total\# of clients last year}}$	A high churn rate indicates that many clients tend to leave you at the end of the year. This means you will need to work harder next year to replace the clients you've lost. Knowing this metric will help you better understand how to forecast your revenue and client engagements. If you have high client churn, look for opportunities to embed and expand.

Metric	How to calculate	Implications/Application
Average Tenure of Clients	Count the # of years your clients continuously hire you and take an average across your clients	The longer your clients stay with you, the more you're embedded with them and demonstrating your value. If you have a long list of clients, count only the ones who meet a meaningful revenue threshold.
Annual Number of Referrals	Count # of referrals received each year (solicited and unsolicited)	This metric measures how successful you are in gaining referrals. The longer you are in business, the more referrals you should be receiving each year. Note your top referrers.
Buyer Quality	$$\frac{\text{Revenue}}{\text{\# of buyers}}$$	A low revenue per buyer may signal you have too many clients and may be spreading yourself too thin. You can increase this metric by up-selling or cross-selling your services.
Revenue Growth per Customer Over a Three-Year Rolling Period	$(((\text{revenue of latest full year} \div \text{revenue from earliest year})^{\wedge}(1/3)) - 1)*100$	(For the rainmaking quants) This metric will measure your success rate establishing yourself with a client. For newer clients, you'll want to see a higher percentage because you likely have more room to grow as you move from embed to expand.

END OF PART II:
Strategies Matter

When it comes to strategies, keep in mind two quotes from the heavy hitters of their day. The first is one often attributed to writer, scientist, diplomat, and US founding father Benjamin Franklin: "By failing to prepare, you are preparing to fail." The second comes from an actual heavy hitter, former heavyweight boxing champ Mike Tyson: "Everybody has a plan until they get punched in the mouth."

If you approach business development haphazardly, you may run out of time, patience, or interest to keep selling before you see real success. By internalizing the strategies in this part and using the right one based on your client scenario, you can make the most of your rainmaking efforts. Each strategy sets the intent and end goal for your actions: generating revenue by serving your clients well. To help you build up a healthy book of business, you'll want to *stay top of mind* to find real needs, *instill confidence* to close opportunities when a need presents itself, and *expand your reach* to uncover additional needs and become the go-to advisor. Work these business development strategies daily, and as you use them, refine and evolve them to best fit you, your clients, and your firm's offerings. Whenever you're unsure about your next business-development step with an Ideal Connection, come back to Part II for some ideas.

These strategies act as a map to your destination, but you'll still need the right tactics, or skills, to navigate the road. Like Iron Mike reminds us, a plan only gets us so far. You must adjust your approach based on what's happening in front of you. To execute these strategies well, while being flexible to manage the unexpected, you need more than just a plan. Sun Tzu, the ancient Chinese military strategist, supposedly said, "Strategy without tactics is the slowest route to victory. Tactics without strategy is the noise before defeat." To put these strategies to best use, you need to sharpen your rainmaking skills. It's one thing to know where you're going, and it's another to actually get there.

Tactics

Though adopting the rainmaker's mindset and strategies helps you set the stage for success, you still need to step up on that stage and perform. That's where tactics come in. Rainmaking tactics are the observable skills you use to successfully sell your expertise. You might have noticed the importance of actively listening when you shadowed your more senior colleagues. Perhaps you attended a sales training workshop that focused on managing objections. You may have heard advice from a panel of your leaders that emphasized networking and keeping your pipeline full.

It's easy to learn a tactic here, pick up a tactic there, but without understanding how they fit together, or how you get better at them, you'll be stuck with a mixed bag of disconnected, underdeveloped skills that will limit your rainmaking potential. To enhance your effectiveness as a rainmaker, you'll want to regularly develop and use a set of core tactics that allow you to manage the various interactions you'll have when building your book of business. And although a whole book could be written on rainmaking tactics, there are five that will carry you throughout your career:

- **Build a trusted reputation:** Your reputation is the foundation on which you build your book of business—the stronger the foundation, the bigger the book of business.

- **Communicate care, competence, collaboration:** The decision to hire you will heavily depend on the experience you give your prospects throughout your interactions. Effective communication is the tactic you use to craft that experience.

- **Drive the process forward:** Rarely will sales just happen on their own. You need to get the conversation going, keep the momentum, and overcome obstacles that get in the way.

- **Protect your rainmaking time:** How you spend your time will determine the results you achieve. Protecting and maximizing your time with the contacts on your Ideal Connections' list will help you generate revenue in a sustainable, long-term way.

- **Stay relevant:** To keep up with your clients' evolving needs, you'll need to innovate your approach and be adept at learning. Knowing how to effectively develop yourself equips you with the tactics to adapt and be resilient to an ever-changing landscape.

As with any skill, these tactics take effort to build, but look effortless when mastered. You'll have some that will come easy, while others may prove more difficult. As long as you stay in the growth mindset while being realistically optimistic about your current skill level, you can learn these tactics.

It's important to recognize that tactics are learned by doing, not through intellectual understanding. You've likely heard of or even learned some of these tactics before, and most, if not all, should sound like common sense—but common sense is not always common practice. To master these tactics, you'll need to practice them consistently, incorporating them in your daily interactions whenever possible. At the end of each chapter, you'll find practical ways to use and refine these tactics.

CHAPTER

9

Build a Trusted Reputation

Chapter 9: Build a Trusted Reputation

Early in his career, Jason Trennert, Chairman and CEO of the institutional research firm Strategas Securities, noticed the research analysts who struggled to market their research were those who thought their insights alone would be enough to bring in business. He contrasts that perspective with what he had learned from his mentor, Ed Hyman, considered one of Wall Street's greatest economists.[1] According to Trennert, Hyman emphasized that "analysts have to be very strong advocates for their own work. You cannot rely on other people to be your best advocate, but you can help other people advocate on your behalf."

Not only did Hyman do much of the economic research and analysis, but he also took the initiative to actively share his research reports with his sales team. They took notice and invited him to join them in their client meetings. Despite doing most of the technical heavy-lifting, Hyman was the first to get on a plane to go visit clients or pick up the phone when they called. He built his reputation at his organization and across his industry by proactively marketing his expertise and building his network. Trennert experienced Hyman's approach in real-time, then later applied this philosophy in growing his own firm. He trains his research analysts to pitch their work both internally and externally. From Hyman, Trennert learned that you are responsible for your own success.

As much as you would like others on their own to notice your expertise and recognize your value, most people are just not paying attention to you. To pique their interest, you'll want to actively advocate for your work and develop a strong brand. Once people see, understand, and value what you do, they'll keep you in mind if they think you can either help them or help someone in their network. The more people know what you're capable of, and the more they connect with you, the more likely they'll recommend you to others in their network. To increase your chances of being recommended, your first step is to increase your visibility and draw the attention of your Ideal Connections.

Maybe they stumble upon you online, meet you in person, see you speak, read one of your articles, or hear about you from one of their close contacts. Once your Ideal Connections are paying attention to you, you'll want to deepen their positive impression of you and help them understand how you might help them, their colleagues, and other people they know. Some people might call this networking, marketing, or personal branding, but whatever the label, it boils down to building your reputation.

Your reputation works for you while you sleep. It sells for you when you're not there. It grows as others talk about you in the marketplace, for good and for bad. Take ownership of your reputation. The more effective you are at building a trusted brand, the higher your chances of being hired and referred to others. As you work with and engage more people, your network widens and your reputation grows, further helping you win deals and learn about new opportunities. A strong network and brand are critical—when it comes to building our book of business over the long-term, we all need as much help as we can get.

The True Value of Networking

I know. I know. You've heard it ad nauseum from your boss, colleagues, and consultants, and you've even reminded yourself: "You need to network." When most people hear this, they immediately react with a sigh or groan, maybe even a bit of a shudder. Most of us prefer working to net-working. Some even see networking as *not working*, something to do when you have extra time or when you're looking for a new job. But for rainmakers, effective networking is an essential part of their work. And when you're building your book of business, it becomes equally, if not more important than your technical work. A trusted reputation will reward you with not only inbound opportunities, but a higher rate of success in closing those opportunities.

Your Network Makes You More Valuable

Many of us think of networking as just meeting people; in reality, effective networking is teaching others the value we can offer to them. In addition to the value of our expertise, the more powerful our network, the more valuable we are to others. As discussed in Chapter 8, when your clients and prospects discover the strength of your network, they recognize they're not only tapping into your expertise, but also your access to people who could be integral to their success. Figure 9.1 shows a visual depiction of two people's networks, Antonio's and Maria's. The person icon in the middle represents Antonio and Maria and the dots represent

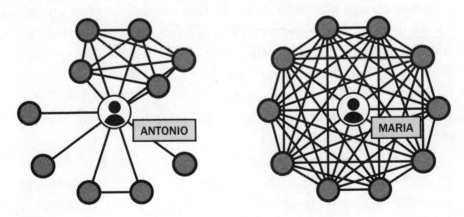

FIGURE 9.1 Whose Network Gives More Power?

a person in their network. Each line shows a relationship between two people in the network. Comparing these two networks, whose do you think is more powerful?

Most people normally choose Maria's. The lattice structure looks strong, and the lines seem to imply interconnection, which in theory would create a more powerful and robust network. But the strength of your network, and the value supplied, should not be judged by how connected everyone is to each other; it should be judged by the role you play in that network.

Consider what happens when Antonio and Maria are removed from their networks. Maria's is typical of someone whose network mostly consists of their colleagues at work, or a group of close-knit friends. Everyone already knows each other, so Maria doesn't add unique value to that network. In contrast, Antonio is able to connect different groups of people who wouldn't have met without him. By being at the heart of the network, Antonio can provide access to these different groups, making him more valuable to everyone.

Most of our networks will naturally look like Maria's. We tend to develop deeper relationships with people around us, and those people develop their relationships in the same circles. Though that network may expand, if we also connect with people in other groups and networks, not just immediate ones around us, we increase our value to everyone. To diversify and grow your networks, find ways to vary the events you attend and the groups you join. Then, look to become the "node" between different networks. Not only will this make you more valuable, you'll also widen your own knowledge base, and your reputation in other circles will ripple out as well.[2]

As you meet more and more people, keep track of the ones you genuinely connect with. Not only will they be responsive to you, they'll also be more willing to help you and consistently follow through on their promises to do so. These people will be important to building your reputation as they are likely to refer business to you, pass your name to others, and generally speak highly of you. When you come across these special connections, take the lead to solidify your relationship. Show urgency and follow through on your offers to help them. Introduce them to prospective clients; inform them about trends in their industry; invite them to relevant conferences; coach them on a difficult interaction; connect them with a potential collaborator; or encourage them when they're down. The list of ways you can help is nearly endless; the point is to help often, building up a network that works, now and into the future.

Make Networking Work for You

There are three main components to networking, as outlined in Figure 9.2. You first need to capture people's awareness. Then you need to form a connection so they're willing to learn more about you. Once they're interested in you, you have to demonstrate your value, so they understand how you can help them. When all three of these components come together, your contacts will be increasingly open to working with you.

To start developing awareness, make sure to communicate your brand in the right forums. Take a few minutes right now and review your list of Ideal Connections. Are there specific places where they gather, whether online or in person? For example, if you're a banker looking to connect with private equity partners in the healthcare sector, you may want to attend the J.P. Morgan Health Care Conference. If you're an accountant looking to connect with CFOs, you might think about the MIT Sloan CFO summit or AICPA & CIMA CFO Conference. If you're a lawyer looking to connect with entrepreneurs and VCs, you might explore and join a few online forums.

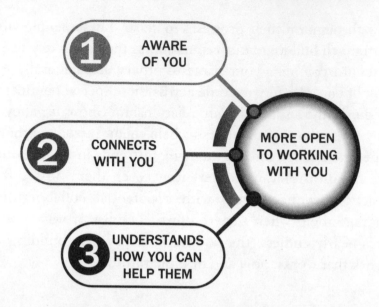

FIGURE 9.2 Critical Components of Networking

Next, choose a forum that plays to your specific strengths, personality, and interests (as explored in Chapter 2). If you're better communicating and connecting one-on-one, schedule coffee or lunch with your Ideal Connections to build up your network. If you're more effective on stage in front of a crowd, you'll want to book conference talks with trade groups relevant to your industry and services. Or if the written word can best showcase your abilities, you might write articles and books that showcase your expertise, or a column for a credible publication your Ideal Connections read.

One of my colleagues had to rebuild her network from scratch when she moved from Singapore to Silicon Valley. To jumpstart connections in her new location, she hosted Saturday brunches and facilitated lively dinner discussions with COOs,

VPs, and senior women leaders in tech. These leaders loved meeting each other and enjoyed the insightful conversations, and now they're more than just clients—they've become some of her best friends. If you're not sure what to do, try on different approaches and figure out which activities you can sustain that drive results for you. (Speaking of driving results, I know of a consultant who started a carpool into the city with other professionals in his area as a way to network.)

Another way to pinpoint the right networking activity for you is to find out how your recent clients heard about you and your firm. If your service is one that most people find through an online search, then you'll want to explore digital marketing services and search-term ads. If many of your clients come to your company after attending a talk from one of your colleagues, or from reading one of your detailed research reports, then you'll want to invest more time delivering talks and writing. No matter the medium, start today. Like compounding interest, where incremental deposits over time lead to large results, starting early and networking consistently will help you achieve sizeable gains to your reputation. A great place to begin is "at home," within your organization.

Network Inside Out

When your colleagues are aware of you, connect well with you, and understand how you can help them, they'll be more interested in working with you, leading to new opportunities. So, one of the best places to build your reputation is internally, especially if you work at a larger organization. In some ways, it's easier because you already share a common affiliation with your co-workers— after all, you work at the same company. Your bosses—whether managers, senior partners, or executives—have an interest in your success. If you show you're trustworthy, driven, and capable of taking care of the firm's clients, you'll likely be considered to support different client opportunities as they arise.

If you do well with these client opportunities by demonstrating emotional intelligence, strong execution, and client service skills, your leaders may elevate your role within the relationship. By remaining visible, and demonstrating a willingness to help, you increase your chances of being considered for inbound leads and active client engagements. Make a point to advocate for yourself to your business development team and your senior colleagues. Some of your more tenured colleagues might have more clients than they can manage, others may be retiring and are looking to transition their clients. Keep an eye out for these opportunities. By helping others manage their client "overflow," you allow them to focus on their key clients while building up your own book of business.

When you offer to help your rainmakers with their clients, don't expect anything in return. Actively share solutions and approaches you've developed for one client that may be useful for your colleagues. To be appointed a lead for key projects, put in the work to own not just the process with your clients but the relationship with them as well. As you build a reputation of being reliable, resourceful, and ready to work, you'll attract your senior colleagues' attention. Once you do, they'll find opportunities to pull you into their engagements, positioning you as a potential successor for their clients. When it's time for them to retire or move on, they'll have confidence in transitioning their clients to you. (Of course, be sensitive to the clients your partners may not be ready to transition away.)

You'll know you're headed in the right direction when senior colleagues specifically request you on their engagement teams, or when you start getting recognized for your work, such as through promotions and bonuses. However, if no one knows who you are, such opportunities aren't going to come your way.

To get their attention, you have to engage in networking activities that continue to grow your brand and reputation. Even within the same company, you'll be more valuable if you can become the node for different groups within your organization. Whether you're building your brand internally or externally, you'll want to use the following tactics to make the most out of these common networking settings.

Navigating Live Events, Conferences, and Trade Shows

When it comes to in-person or virtual gatherings, most people approach and participate in these networking events from the perspective of an attendee. But unless you're great at working a room and chatting up strangers, you may want to consider other options that can equally, if not more effectively, help you network at live events. Table 9.1 provides an overview of these potential roles, the networking upsides and downsides to each one, and practical tips on how to approach them. As you learn about each role, assess the ones that would best fit your styles and strengths. There may be more than one, and it's possible that certain roles may feel more comfortable to you depending on the specific event and attendees.

Your goal at these live events is to quickly and authentically connect with others so that you can continue your conversation after the event. A fast way to get a dialogue started is to initiate the conversation. You might start by introducing yourself, followed by a question or comment regarding the immediate surroundings. For example, "Hi, my name is Robert Chen from Exec|Comm. How do you like the conference so far?" Find questions that will help spark a connection and keep the conversation going. Instead of asking "What do you do?" ask, "Where are you coming in from?" or "What do you love to do?"[3] to potentially tap into non-business-related and more distinctive responses.

Table 9.1   Networking at Live Events

Role	Networking Upside	Networking Downside	Practical Tip
Event organizer or chair	• Access to VIP events, speakers, and volunteers • Chance to network with other leaders • Provides elevated status, making it easier to approach strangers as the event host	• Major commitment that may take time away from other networking opportunities • Requires organizational skills	Find a way to connect others together through your insider knowledge, helping you to build your network beyond the event. Shape the type of events that play to your strength and use your role to recruit sponsors, speakers, and volunteers you want to meet.
Volunteer	• Access to VIP events and speakers • Chance to network with other volunteers and event leaders • Volunteer status makes it easier to approach strangers	• Depending on your role, you may not have time to actually network at the event • You may get stuck with a role that does not give the best first impression	Take on a volunteer role that gives you networking value. Don't just say, "I'll do anything." Pick a volunteer role that showcases your strengths while adding value to the event.
Moderator	• Able to connect with the speakers before, during, and after the session • Good visibility with attendees	• Typically, not in a position to showcase your individual expertise	Choose to moderate a panel of speakers you want to connect with. Set up a call to get to know everyone, and follow-up afterward. Don't try to steal the spotlight—your job is to keep the discussion relevant and to make the panelists look good.

Role	Networking Upside	Networking Downside	Practical Tip
Speaker	• High visibility and great platform to demonstrate your expertise. People will usually approach you after your talk if you did well • Depending on your comfort level with speaking, doesn't take a lot of time to prepare, and you can repurpose previous talks • Depending on the speaker lineup, your inclusion can provide social proof of your expertise	• Big conferences sometimes require you to pay to be given stage time • You need to be good in this medium or else it can backfire bigtime	Tell your contacts where you'll be speaking. They may want to attend, and even if they can't, it's a great way of educating them about the value others see in you. Offer to lead breakout sessions that will attract your Ideal Connections so you can connect more intimately with attendees. When speaking on a panel, make sure the other panelists have a strong reputation, so your brand is enhanced by being associated with them.
Attendee	• Freedom to decide whom to speak with and how to spend your time (including leaving early if needed!) • Can enjoy the event without other responsibilities • Can leverage event to build your knowledge and gain insights you can share with others	• Need to "work the room," often without knowing who's who, leading to wasted time and energy • Hard to demonstrate your value	Arrive early—it's much harder to meet new people if you show up late and everyone is already talking to each other. Also, speakers tend to arrive early to get ready, so you may have a chance to connect with them. Before any event you are attending, reach out to your Ideal Connections and let them know about the event and ask if they were, by any chance, planning to attend. You might also follow up with past attendees as well.

After kicking off the conversation, listen to their response and ask related follow-up questions. When appropriate, share more about yourself, but be brief and reengage the other person with a question. Stay completely present and focused on the other person. Avoid the looking-for-someone-more-interesting-to-talk-to glance over the other person's shoulder—it's not only obvious, but off-putting. As the conversation progresses, you'll want to be ready to pivot to a different topic when the first one fizzles out. Your goal is to hit on a resonant topic of interest and connect on that topic. A good way to keep the conversation going is to remember the acronym FLOW, which stands for family, leisure, organizations, and "what's in the news." If you're not having much luck with one topic, move onto the next one in the FLOW acronym. Take responsibility to keep the conversation "FLOWing." The more genuine curiosity you express in the other person, the more easily common connections will surface.

Once you connect on a common interest, affiliation, or goal, you'll want to wrap up the conversation. Though this may sound counterintuitive, the idea here is to get the conversation to the point where the person you're talking to wants to connect with you beyond the event. Although you can both keep the conversation going for much longer (a sign of a true connection), you don't want to rob each other of the chance to expand your networks. Exchange contact information and decide on a specific timeframe after the event to circle back with each other.

Most people will get this idea, but you'll have others who fear they won't connect with anyone else for the rest of the event, so they may cling to you as their safety blanket. In these situations, it's helpful to know a few ways to gracefully make your exit. You might directly say, "You probably came here to broaden your network. Let's exchange information and grab tea later this month." You can also connect the person with someone else you know at the event to help them both expand their network, especially if the two have some common interests. That said, if you're looking to simply get away because you're not having a great experience, introducing them to a contact might not be the best move—you don't want your contacts feeling like you've saddled them with a less than ideal conversation (to put it nicely).

If you have a real clinger, you may need to take more drastic action. Excuse yourself to refill your drink, make a call, or go to the restroom. Whatever reason you give, make sure you actually do what you say you have to do. You don't want to tell someone you're heading to the restroom, then get caught immediately joining another group's conversation. Remember, you're looking to build a positive reputation—even if you don't gel with someone, you don't want to come across as rude or insincere. The last thing you want out of a networking event is to get badmouthed by someone you inadvertently offended.

After the event, add any new Ideal Connections you met to your sales follow-up system, as introduced in Chapter 6. Then make sure to follow up—the actual networking activity doesn't yield fruit unless you continue the conversation, deepen the connection, and teach this individual how you're able to add value. You can follow up by connecting on LinkedIn, setting up a coffee meeting, or making other plans to get together. If you speak at an event, decide how you'll stay in touch with the attendees. Invite them to reach out to you, sign up for your newsletter, or connect with you online.

Craft Your Online Presence

Take a moment right now and look yourself up online. What did you find? Does the information that first pops up—the websites, social media accounts, articles, and videos—reflect the brand qualities you want others to associate with you? Based on what you see, would you hire yourself? Maybe your LinkedIn profile comes up as the first search result. If you received a connection request from yourself on LinkedIn, based on the quality of your profile, would you immediately say "yes" to connecting, or would it give you pause? Most people will look you up online before they decide whether or not to engage with you. That means the first impression you make today comes from your online presence and the content accessible online, whether blog posts, videos, or even comments on other people's posts.

When people have a positive first impression of you, they will likely interpret your subsequent actions in a positive light. In some cases, we don't have control over our first impressions, but when it comes to our online presence, we can craft it in a way that highlights our expertise, value, and authenticity from the start. People want to connect with other *real* people, not just those who are talented, but those who are interesting and likable. Showing a more personal side to what is likely a strong professional side can help. For example, on my LinkedIn headline, I highlight my status as a "semi-cool dad" to counterbalance my professional credentials. In general, people are suspicious when they find someone online who seems too polished.

Your online presence should match your reality, and help people envision how you might help them. You might showcase testimonials, case studies, and your thought leadership pieces. Even if you only get ten views on a video right now, or only a handful of likes on a blog post, as you continue to enhance your brand, you'll find that more people will discover your body of work. Boost your credibility by including career milestones, awards, and other professional accolades on your bio and social media profiles. Your online presence can also signal to others how well you're connected. For example, If people can see a number of high-quality connections on LinkedIn or an impressive number of Instagram followers, their impression of you may go up. A strong online network shows you have access to relationships or information to help your clients more effectively.

Creating original content that you can then share across multiple mediums is also important, whether podcasts, written work, or videos. This dynamic content provides a way to refresh your presence with your connections. Some people post regularly on their social media sites or write a column or newsletter that gets sent to their clients periodically. Others engage actively with followers on Twitter or in online forums. You could start a mailing list to keep track of your contacts who want to hear from you and use it to share content you've written or produced. If you write something that is readily accessible for others, you again expand your reach.

Even if you connect more effectively live, you should still build up online brand assets that will work for you, twenty-four-seven, without your active involvement. You can record snippets of talks you've given, spreading your ideas to a wider audience and increasing the longevity of your content (all without your involvement after it's posted). Find ways to capture timeless content, which will be useful no matter how much time has passed since you first posted it. You don't want to just post material that will become irrelevant moments later, nor do you want to spend all your time tinkering with your online profiles. This evergreen content does the work of communicating your expertise and connecting with others, "networking for you" so you can focus on other reputation-building avenues. Whatever approach you take, though, decide on the medium you're most comfortable with and make sure to consistently get in front of your Ideal Connections.

Practice the Tactics

- Write down the names of your five closest professional contacts.

  ○ How connected are these contacts to each other? Does your network resemble Antonio's or Maria's?

  ○ How many people on this list have referred business to you?

  ○ What's one way you can teach these five people how you can add value to them and their network?

- Connect two people in your network who would appreciate meeting each other.

- Analyze how your current clients typically find you or your firm. Is it through word of mouth, at events, or through the thought leadership your firm has put out there?

- For your next live event, consider the different roles you could potentially play and choose the one that best fits you.

- Strike up a conversation with an internal colleague you don't know and find a connection point. You might want to start with, "What group are you in and what are you working on?" and then keep the conversation FLOWing until you find a common interest or affiliation.

- Find a way to help your boss or a rainmaking senior colleague with one of their client engagements with no expectation that they will compensate or pass this client to you.
- If you haven't done so already, look yourself up online and find one aspect to improve about your online presence.

Communicate Care, Competence, Collaboration

Chapter 10: Communicate Care, Competence, Collaboration

When two people sit down to talk, they each know what they want to get out of the interaction. For example, Abdul might be looking to grow his network and learn more about a new industry, and Olga might want to uncover a need she and her firm can help solve. Each of them will likely try to take the conversation in the direction they want it to go. Abdul might start by asking how Olga got into her current role, while Olga tries to learn more about the key focus for Abdul's firm. Throughout the conversation, they keep going back and forth, each nudging the topics toward their desired direction. Like most people, Abdul and Olga are not thinking about whether the other person actually wants to go where they are trying to take them.

Although it is good to know what you're looking to accomplish, it is equally important, if not more so, to be tuned into what the other person wants from the interaction. It's important to think about their goals for meeting with you, and remain present during the meeting, to ensure you create a positive experience for them. By helping them accomplish what they want out of the conversation, you'll find that they'll be more open to helping you achieve your goals in return. True communication takes place when you care about what the other person has to say, display your competence in your ability to help them, and collaborate throughout the interaction to find value for both of you.

At this point in your career, you may have gone through a fair amount of training covering communication skills cornerstones, such as active listening and presentation techniques. As you develop your rainmaker tactics, you need to continue practicing these core communication skills and adeptly apply them in the moment to create a client-centric experience. Effective communication respects others' time and uses it wisely, and it is a must-have in building trust and long-term relationships. When professionals first shift to business development, they often tend to be too talkative. They feel the need to pitch and persuade the other person and also to demonstrate their expertise. Sometimes they're on the other side of the spectrum, asking too many questions, trying hard to show how good they are at listening, without driving the conversation forward (the purgatory of never-ending discovery). Neither way is effective. Instead, you want to know when to listen and when to talk, and how to do both well.

To discern whether to listen or to talk, you'll first need to understand how to read the room and gauge whether the other person in the conversation feels their time is being well spent. Once it's clear, you will either listen with empathy or speak with confidence so your Ideal Connections feel assured that your relationship will become a partnership. By communicating in such a way, you keep the interaction focused on them, ensuring they feel heard when they speak. When the other person recognizes you're truly listening to them, they will not only be encouraged to open up and share their needs in more detail, they will also be more open to what you have to say. A clear two-way communication channel will be both the indicator and the linchpin of a successful collaboration.

Read the Room

In any prospect or client interaction, it pays to plan ahead, but no matter how well you prepare, conversations won't always go the way you expect. The other person may react in a way you hadn't considered, or a key stakeholder may be invited last minute without notice. To help you navigate these unforeseen situations, be ready to manage your prospects' and clients' real-time reactions (not to mention your own). To do so, you need to stay aware, proactively reading the room at all times. The details you observe live during any conversation are cues to help you better communicate with the other person, adjusting as needed to keep them engaged.

During any meeting, you don't want to ask yourself "How am I doing?" Instead, answer the question "How is the other person reacting?" If you place too much attention on your own performance, you will lose sight of the other person and their needs. Whenever you're in a live interaction, focus on what's happening in the moment, taking in details about the person in the room, the surroundings, and the interaction itself.

Read the Person

Before your meeting, prime yourself to be client-focused. Think about the client's role and priorities, your relevance to them, and the reason they are willing to speak with you. By understanding who you are dealing with, you'll have a better chance of making the interaction worthwhile for them. And the more value they receive from the conversation, the more likely they will escalate their commitment to you (as discussed in Chapter 6).

Just as the other person will size you up when they first meet you, you'll want to size them up as well. Pay attention to the language they use, their appearance, and their overall communication style. Ask yourself what they're consciously or unconsciously communicating. If they overuse jargon, is that because they see themselves as a subject matter expert and want everyone to know it? Or are they so used to working with internal folks that they don't recognize they're using specialized terms? If you think they see themselves as a subject matter expert, you might consult their opinion throughout the interaction.

Note their appearance. Does it reveal an attention to detail, a desire to conform, or pride in being unconventional? Based on what you observe, you may better interpret what you are hearing, allowing you to formulate a more fitting response. For example, if the other person talks about "disrupting their business," and sports a t-shirt that says, "Apple Macintosh 1984,"[1] you might offer some of your more innovative offerings that would be less palatable for traditional clients who might prefer to stick with your core services.

Anna Mok, Global Lead Client Service Partner and Senior Advisory Partner at a Big Four Accounting Firm and President and Executive Board Chair of Ascend Leadership, suggests quickly assessing the person you're speaking with to figure out their communication preferences. Being responsible for the Asia Pacific region and having spent decades leading clients around the world Anna notes, "When you are interacting with someone, if they are no nonsense and don't want to waste time with pleasantries, get right down to business. If they want to know you as a human and see you in a different light, you need to recognize that, and understand where they're coming from." These preferences will give you insight into how the person will feel most comfortable interacting with you.

We all have a preferred style of communication. When others adopt our preferred style, we feel like they get what we're saying. People who are analytical and detailed oriented, for example, can easily mislabel someone as lacking substance if they tend to only support their arguments with anecdotal evidence. Those who are focused on the big picture and on relationships may see someone diving deep into data as being stuck in the weeds. If the other person wants to drive the agenda, talk less. If you're not flexing to their style, you may both try to grab airtime and end up interrupting or talking over each other. If you naturally default to listening, but the other person wants you to lead the interaction, you need to do so. Otherwise, you may end up with some awkward silences as each of you wait for the other to lead the conversation. When you're not sure about the other person's tendencies, be ready to engage in friendly chit-chat in case they want to go there, and lead with your main message upfront. As the conversation unfolds, you'll take their cues to decide what to do next.

Read the Surroundings

Your surroundings may provide clues to how the other person sees this interaction or their relationship to you. For example, if they invite you to a boardroom for your first meeting and sit across the table from you, the interaction is likely to be more formal than if they asked you to grab coffee at the local cafe. You likely don't have a great relationship with someone who suggests meeting for fifteen minutes in their lobby instead of offering to go for lunch at their favorite restaurant. Sometimes, the surroundings can give you insights into the other person and what they value. If you're invited to their office and see diplomas and awards prominently displayed on the walls, you may want to be ready to talk about your credentials. If the room is filled with family photos and inspirational quotes, you might want to pay closer attention to how you are connecting with each other on a more personal level.

Read the Interaction

Pay attention to how the other person is responding to the interaction. If your Ideal Connection is nodding, asking relevant questions, and leaning in, you know your approach is working and you can stay the course. A raised or furrowed brow may signal confusion or skepticism, in which case, you might want to pause and check in to see if there are any questions or concerns. If you find the other person beginning to disengage with you—stealing a glance at their watch or phone, impatiently tapping their pen, or giving short responses—you might take a moment to reset by saying, "Are we on the right track here? What are your thoughts on what you've heard so far, and are we missing anything at this point?"

No matter what you *think* the other person wants from the interaction, you will be more on point when you actually *ask* them what they want in real time. Build space using proactive check-ins throughout the interaction. One of the best times to start is right after you share the purpose for the conversation. For example, immediately after you say, "I appreciate your time today to discuss X" ask, "Before we begin, what would be most helpful to discuss?" You might also ask, "Has anything changed since our last meeting?" You'll want to know upfront if your client has a pressing concern they would like to discuss or a new development that is material to the conversation.

Though you will know where you want to go in the interaction, don't let your preparation or expectations for the conversation create tunnel vision. Ascend's Anna Mok has seen this unfortunate situation happen often. "I've been in so many meetings when people just get stuck to the script, instead of shifting gears when the client tells them something different than what they had rehearsed for." She continues, "They were just so focused on what they wanted to say, they ultimately forgot that they had to listen to the client. We have to listen to the cues."

When you hear these cues, adjust accordingly so you take the conversation in the direction the other person wants to go. In addition to checking in at the start of the meeting, you'll want to create space to hear from the other person throughout the interaction. Try inserting breaks throughout the discussion to ask, "What are your thoughts so far?" or "How does that sound?" By checking in, you keep the conversation relevant and focused on the other person's needs. These cues will also provide insight into when you should be listening and when you should be talking. Recognizing the difference is a necessary part of successfully navigating any conversation.

Know When to Listen and When to Talk

As you plan for the interaction, consider the other person's goals and expectations for the conversation. If your client is looking to vet you, for example, they may want you to talk more so they can learn what they need to in an effort to assess you more fully. But if you avoid giving substantive answers and keep asking them questions about their situation, they may discount your credibility. Though you're just trying to fully understand their situation, they may misinterpret your ongoing questioning as a lack of experience or familiarity with their issue. They'll likely assume you don't know how to address their problem and either express their frustration or cut short the conversation. Conversely, when your prospect or client comes to you with a need, they may have a lot of information to share, and they will want to make sure you listen more as they explain the context and nuances of the problem they're up against. From their perspective, by listening, you instill confidence that you have a good understanding of their situation before sharing your thoughts.

When you're not sure of the other person's expectation, lead with listening. We often feel compelled to talk because we want to drive the agenda. What's powerful about listening, though, is that it allows us to take the guesswork out of deciphering what the other person wants. "Leading with listening," however, doesn't mean being passive and just sitting there looking interested. As you're listening, you'll need to actively manage your reactions to what you hear so the other person feels encouraged to continue talking. You'll want to ask follow-up questions to show you're engaged and use them to help control the flow of the conversation. The more you listen, the more you learn (and you won't learn anything new if you're the only one talking). The better you understand what the other person is looking to accomplish, the more effective you'll be in helping them.

Listen with Empathy

In conversations with prospects and clients, you're not just trying to learn new information, you're also attempting to find out how the other person feels about the situation. This type of empathetic listening doesn't have a hidden agenda, and it's not done to guide the other person down a specific path—it's wholly meant to keep the focus on them so you can fully understand their perspective. When people recognize you're listening to them with empathy, and without judgment, they will be more open and candid with their responses.

In most cases, manage the conversation by answering questions succinctly, then end your response with a question in return. This approach puts the spotlight back on the other person. You learn more, and they feel heard and respected. Start your conversations with open-ended questions. They usually begin with a "what," "how," or "why" and cannot be answered with a simple "yes" or "no." (If you're not good at managing your tone, you may want to stay away from "why" questions since they may sound accusatory.) For example:

- "*What* makes this an important priority for you?"
- "*How* have you addressed this in the past?"
- "*Why* are you focused on this issue now?"

Again, these questions invite the person you're speaking with to open up based on how they see the issue—not how you frame it. Contrast "What makes this an important priority for you?" with, "Is this a priority for you because you're looking to grow your company?" This second, close-ended question could limit what the other person would have shared. By framing the question around the idea of them looking to grow their company, you may inadvertently get them focused on that idea, even though they might have other reasons that makes this issue a high priority. An additional benefit of this approach is that it puts you in control of the conversation—as mentioned, the person asking the questions dictates the topic of conversation.

As discussed in Chapter 7, as you're listening, you may hear something similar to other situations you've handled with other clients, and you may be tempted to let the person know that you've handled their problem before. Take a beat and keep listening. Treat what they say as unique to them. Though the problem or challenge may be the same to others you've successfully addressed, your client's context and experience will be different, which is, of course, what makes their challenge unique.

More than that, they want to tell their story. They have likely been struggling with their issue for months—if not years—and it'll be hard for them to believe that after speaking with them for a few minutes you already have the solution. Even if you've heard the same story hundreds of times, let them share their experience. If you quickly bucket what you hear as "another one of those," your clients will assume you will give them some boilerplate solution. Not only might that result in lower fee expectations, but this will also stunt your growth with your client. If you don't really listen to what they're saying and assume you've "seen it all before," then you likely won't be able to provide them with what they truly need. You're creating a more transactional relationship as opposed to a true partnership.

The fact is you have relevant experience that may help this new client. The way to demonstrate that expertise is to ask great questions that show you understand the key issues the client is raising, not to interrupt and push solutions on them. There will be time for solutions—and more targeted ones—after you've listened better to what's really going on with your client.

To help ensure you're on the same page with your client, play back what you've heard. By playing back your interpretation of what was said, you will get one of three responses. The other person can respond with "yes," confirming you're on the right track and you've made them feel heard. They might say "no" and go on to clarify what they really meant, helping you gain new information. They might also say "yes and. . ." and go on to share even more information that you might have missed if you hadn't played back what you had heard. By confirming you're both on the same page, you'll be more able to keep the conversation and your follow-up questions and responses relevant to your client.

To keep an open channel of communication, employ the physical and verbal signals of non-judgmental listening laid out in Table 10.1.

Another way to ensure you're listening with empathy is to catch any knee-jerk responses that show you're not listening.

Table 10.1   Physical and Verbal Signs of Non-Judgmental Listening

Physical Signs	Verbal Signs
• Maintain strong eye contact to show you're paying attention—don't steal looks at your phone or email.	• Confirm or play back what you've heard.
• Match facial expression to what you're hearing.	• Ask follow-up questions related to what was just said.
• When appropriate, jot down key points.	• Comment and add value based on what you've heard.
• Nod in a measured way; keep arms apart and hands open to show you're open to what you're hearing.	• Encourage them to keep talking; try saying "Tell me more" or "Can you expand on that?"
• Naturally pace your questions.	• Stay silent after asking a question.

Resist interrupting the other person or turning the conversation back to your agenda. When you hear something you don't agree with, fight the natural urge to defend or explain the counterargument. (Listening intently and letting the other person talk doesn't mean you're agreeing with them.) Avoid giving unsolicited advice like, "Have you tried. . ." or asking judgmental or leading follow-up questions like, "Why did you. . ."

Anytime you catch yourself thinking, "That doesn't make sense" or "Why is this person being so unreasonable?" take note. Typically, when someone makes a statement that we find unreasonable or incorrect, we tend to discount it and move on. When we do so, however, we miss an opportunity to learn more about that person and how they see their situation. If we instead listen closely in these moments, we will have a better chance of bridging their perspective and ours and finding a way to work together. When something doesn't make sense to us, it reveals a gap in our knowledge and expectations. By challenging our own assumptions, we may learn something about the other person that can help further enhance our ability to collaborate with them.

The insights gained through listening will allow you to better address their real need and position your solution in their frame of reference. When my colleagues and I teach listening skills, we remind our clients that the end goal of listening is not only to learn something you didn't know; it is to demonstrate enormous respect for the other person's experience and point of view—a solid foundation of any relationship.

Practical Tip

To keep the other person talking, repeat the last one to three words they've just said.[2] You'll find the other person will likely elaborate from there.

Speak with Confidence and Conviction

We tend to trust people who trust themselves.[3] Their confidence inspires confidence in others. So, whenever we open our mouths in an interaction, we want to do so in a way that signals our trust and confidence in ourselves. You may have the best solution to a prospect's problem, but if you cannot communicate it confidently, then they may discount your idea and your competence.

Warren Buffett recommends developing your communication skills because it "helps to get others to follow your ideas." He goes on to emphasize that "a relatively modest improvement can make a major difference in your future earning power, as well as in many other aspects of your life."[4] Research supports the idea that soft-skills training, such as on communication skills, can increase total sales.[5] Rainmakers recognize this fact, and train themselves to become better communicators. Being an effective communicator means minimizing the other person's ability to misinterpret the conversation. Their misinterpretation can come from both the words you say and the way you say them. Be thoughtful in the way you communicate because others will assume whatever you're saying is being said on purpose.

To project confidence and conviction, you must first understand what people need to see and hear from you to perceive you in that way. In one culture, that might mean taking your space at the table by sitting up tall with expansive body language, sustaining eye contact, and speaking more definitively by coming to a full stop in-between your thoughts. In another culture, it may mean speaking less, and showing deference when discussing your ideas. Definitions of confidence evolve over time as well. To be a strong communicator, expand your range so you can successfully recognize and execute the different behaviors that equate to confidence.

When it is your turn to talk, keep your messages concise, relevant, and substantive:

- **Concise:** Use as many words as needed to make your key point, and no more. Usually, one or two sentences are enough.
- **Relevant:** Every word you say should add value to the conversation. To prepare, imagine the other person asking you, "Why should I care?" in response to each of your key points.
- **Substantive:** You must be able to prove your claims about the value you can create. What compelling evidence can you share that answers the question, "How do you know it works?"

When speaking with prospects, be ready with clear examples told in a way that can help others visualize how they might work with you. You may want to highlight your experience with similar companies, your differentiators, and your results. For example, if you work with logistics companies looking to automate their processes, you might say:

> "Leveraging our expertise in artificial intelligence and machine learning, we help companies like XPO and DHL streamline their parcel monitoring (experience with similar companies). Just last month, we helped another client automate their rate quote system based on our proprietary models and data feeds (differentiator). This change helped them to reduce their labor costs by 12% while driving up revenue for urgent shipments by 27% due to shorter lead times for their customers to receive quotes (results)."

You can also use the classic Problem, Action, and Result (PAR) framework, which can help you substantiate your claims with a deep dive into a specific example. PAR creates a brief outline you can easily remember by recalling a specific example, thinking first of the *problem* you faced, the *action* you performed to solve the problem, and the *result* of your efforts. For example:

> "At Exec|Comm, we work closely with Chief Talent Officers to develop the executive-level skills of their high-performers. An issue that recently came up for our global clients is the high cost of travel expenses to fly US facilitators into their non-US locations (problem). Since we had local resources in their main global hubs, we delivered, simultaneously across 12 countries, a global leadership program for their Executive Directors focused on executive presence, critical thinking, and managing key stakeholders (action). Not only did these programs reduce travel expenses by 35 percent, they also received the highest ratings across the programs offered (result)."

Another way to communicate confidence is to speak with your clients as if they are your peers. Don't talk to them like a consultant. Talk at their level and show you're at ease collaborating with them. For example, if they're executives, you might trade notes on strategic business issues and macro trends impacting their business. With mid-level managers, focus more on the goals related to their functions and performance metrics. During your conversations, project ease by speaking conversationally, staying relaxed, and smiling when appropriate.

Another tactic you'll want to use when it's your turn to talk is to show respect for what the other person brings to the table and avoid seeming like you think you know everything. When sharing your thoughts, assume they may have already considered what you're about to say by using language like, "I suspect you've probably seen a lot of that. . ." or "You likely thought of this already. . . ." When you disagree with what you're hearing, offer your point as an alternative opinion, and position it neutrally, as opposed to appearing more superior than your client's. If the client is insistent on an approach you don't agree with, you can still refuse the work. Try saying, "Based on our experience, I would not be comfortable guiding my team to approach it this way."

Practice the Tactics

- Look at the items on your work desk or a colleague's workspace and determine what you can infer based on what you see. Continue being observant of your surroundings and what they may be able to tell you.

- Choose one of the signs of nonjudgmental listening from Table 10.1 and practice it in every conversation you have this week.

- To gauge your listening skills, ask yourself what you learned in your last conversation with a contact, prospect, or client that you didn't already know. The more you learned, the more you listened.

- Video-record yourself sharing a solution for a recent or upcoming client meeting. Now, as you watch the video, imagine you're the client. Ask yourself:

  - How relevant is the message to what the client cares about?
  - How am I coming across in the way I deliver the information?
  - Do I appear confident and at ease?

- Using the Problem, Action, and Result framework, come up with two specific examples to substantiate your differentiators.

Drive the Process Forward

Chapter 11: Drive the Process Forward

Inertia is the invisible, yet formidable enemy to your business development efforts. It's constantly there, weighing you down and slowing your forward momentum. Inertia never rests. It usually takes less effort to maintain the status quo than to effect change by hiring you. When clients reach out to you with a specific need, no matter how high the need is on their priority list, inertia and other priorities may slow down the process. As a result, you'll want to take ownership for maintaining the momentum and driving the process forward—or else it can easily stand still. Driving the process, though, does not mean being pushy. You still need to focus on what's best for your prospects. You must understand when you can accelerate the process, when you'll need to be patiently persistent, and when there is no way to move forward.

There are many reasons the sales process can stall. Maybe the problem you've been asked to fix has resolved itself. Perhaps your prospect encountered a bigger issue, lost their budget, or simply forgot. Regardless of the reason why the process has halted, you still want to know where you stand at all times and what you can do to advance to a close. Forward momentum doesn't happen on its own. It requires attention, effort, and persistence. Ongoing action is necessary to fight inertia. For any prospect you're pursuing, don't let the momentum stop.

Keep Things in Motion

Like a flywheel, it's easier to keep something in motion when it's already moving. Whenever your prospects show an interest in engaging you, one of your most critical tasks is to keep that momentum going. Once you lose momentum, it will require a lot more effort to get it up and running again. One way to ensure forward motion is to take responsibility for the follow-up. Whether that means scheduling the next meeting at the end of each interaction or finding creative ways to check in with your prospects, you want to make sure you're not putting the ball in their court and waiting for them to reach back out to you.

Our personal preferences color the way we follow up. If you prefer to be given space and don't appreciate proactive follow-ups, you might be reticent to check in with your prospects. Conversely, if you see active check-ins as helpful, you probably follow up with people more frequently. But your preferences aren't what's important here—the frequency and manner in which you reconnect with your prospects should all depend on *their* preference, not yours. Since that's the case, at the start of a relationship, ask your prospects how they would like you to follow up with them. If they don't articulate a preference, it doesn't mean they don't have one; they may just not be experienced working with an external party, so some trial and error may be necessary. Always end a conversation with prospects by asking when you should circle back. This way you're not left debating with yourself after the meeting on when you should follow up.

In some situations, your prospects may go radio silent after an interaction. Don't take it personally. You have no idea what's going on in their lives and where the issue they contacted you about currently stands. Most likely the services you're offering or the problem you're trying to help solve became lower priorities for them. Sometimes people are nonresponsive because they have hired someone else and want to avoid the discomfort of telling you, especially if you've put in a lot of work throughout the process. Maybe the issue is no longer urgent, or they felt the chemistry was off.

To help your prospect feel more at ease to update you on where you stand, consider sending an email acknowledging you've probably lost the business. For example:

> Hi Tom, [something specific] reminded me of the proposal you and I discussed. Since we haven't been able to connect during the last few weeks, I assume you've likely moved in another direction. If that's the case, please let me know, and I hope we'll have another opportunity to work together in the future.

This type of check-in will usually prompt a response. They will either say, "Yes, we've gone with someone else," knowing you'll stop following up with them, or say "no" and give you more guidance on next steps and timing. If they confirm you have lost the business, follow up with "Thank you for considering us. Just so we can continue enhancing your experience with us, what could we have done differently or better?" When it comes to managing your limited time, "yes" or "no" is much better than "maybe." By de-personalizing their nonresponsiveness, you'll find it easier to follow up. Still, even when you follow up at just the right time, and in just the right way, obstacles may still impede your progress.

Overcome Obstacles

When prospects aren't sure about your abilities, they'll likely drag their feet. Perhaps they don't believe your solution will work, or that you're the best person to execute it. They might fear you're charging them too much. Sometimes, they may sense their colleagues becoming less committed to solving the issue. No one wants to be seen as making a poor decision, especially one that is highly visible. It's easier for them to say "no" when they're unsure. Your goal is to ferret out and address these concerns before they say "no" to you, since changing a "no" to a "yes" is usually much more difficult than just nudging someone along who hasn't decided yet.

In your prospecting conversations, listen for hesitancy, concern, or skepticism to uncover potential obstacles. To help you overcome these obstacles, you will need to sharpen two major skills: managing objections and negotiating effectively. By managing objections well, you keep the opportunity alive by persuading prospects to be open to your point of view and showing that you fully understand where they're coming from. When you effectively negotiate, you increase your chances of closing more deals. Both are necessary to turn prospects into clients.

Manage Objections

When prospects push back on your ideas, stay calm. It's natural to get defensive when someone challenges your approach, especially when you're confident about your work and its results. Resist the urge. Recognize that your potential buyer is only challenging your approach because they are engaged with your solution. Their objections indicate interest, and they want to figure out if hiring you is the right decision. (Apathy from a potential buyer is more problematic than push back.)

Objections can indicate your prospects' lack of readiness to move to the next step. They're likely questioning your offering because either they're not clear about the value, or their need is not urgent enough. Objections might also reflect your prospect's attempt to understand how your solution works. If the objection is something minute and focused on working together like "I'm not sure if we'll need all three consultants for this engagement," your prospect has likely bought into working with you, and now they just want to iron out the details. If their objection is, "We don't think an external party can help us solve this issue," you have an uphill climb ahead of you. Resist immediately answering the objection with the rationale for hiring you. Instead, start by more fully understanding their concern and perspective. Once they feel heard, you'll find they are more open to your response to their objection.

Handle objections using the ART framework, as shown in Figure 11.1. (This framework further builds on the communication skills detailed in Chapter 10.)

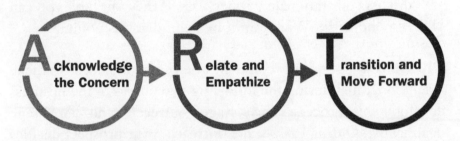

FIGURE 11.1 The ART Process

This three step-process works as follows:

- **Acknowledge:** Don't fight the objection. Acknowledge their perspective by stating the emotions you're observing in them and confirming the issues they've raised. By labeling their emotions, you signal you understand their situation. For example, say, "It sounds like you're concerned about whether we'll be staffing this engagement with a different team than the one you've interacted with so far."

- **Relate:** Look for ways to empathize with your prospect's objections to show you can relate to their position. When possible, inquire further into the objection so they share what's truly on their mind. You can say, "If I were you, I would want to make sure I worked with people I knew and were comfortable with their style. What else concerns you around how we might staff this engagement?" Or try, "Tell us more about your past experiences regarding staffing when you worked with other consulting firms."

- **Transition:** Ask permission to articulate your thoughts on this topic. Find a way to keep the conversation moving forward while remaining respectful. Try leading with the question, "Would it be helpful to hear how we typically decide team staffing and ways we'll actively mitigate the concerns you've just raised?" If they say "yes," you can discuss your rationale to open ears. If they say "no," you can respond with, "What might be helpful at this point?"

Objections typically come up when someone needs to make a decision, often during the following two phases of the business development process: early-stage outreach and late-stage dealmaking. During early-stage outreach, your prospect decides whether to expend their time with you. During late-stage dealmaking, they decide whether to spend their money on you. The more uncertain they are about whether they will get a return for their time or money, the more objections you'll receive. In either situation, the ART framework will come in handy.

In early-stage outreach, especially if you weren't referred or don't have a strong brand, your prospects will likely decline to connect with you. You will be met with a disengaged initial reply like, "We're all set," "Just send me some information," or "I'm not interested." If you're not prepared, you'll respond like most people do to this lack of interest with a simple "OK." But that response is just a reflex. If you truly believe this person would be better off if they had a dialogue with you, then don't settle for "OK." If you are confident about your ability to add value, you need to be prepared to address these common brush-offs so your prospect doesn't lose out on all you have to offer.

Since there isn't much substance to these outreach interactions yet, acknowledging and responding positively with a question can give you another shot at piquing your prospect's interest. For example, if your prospect says:

- "Can you send me information on your company?"
  - Reply, "Happy to do so. Just so we send the most relevant information to you. What are the key priorities you're focused on right now?"
- "I'm heading into a meeting now. Can you call me later?"
  - Reply, "Sure. Happy to do that. Do you want to take a few seconds to pin down a time?"
- "I'm not interested," or "We're busy with X right now"
  - Reply, "Thanks for the candid response. Would you be open to reconnecting in a few months in case anything changes (or when X is done)? Also, would you like us to send you invitations to our upcoming events?"

Notice how each of these responses aims to keep the conversation going either in the moment or at a later point in time. These replies allow you to continue the momentum to build this relationship.

Some prospects you reach out to may already work with someone else who provides services similar to yours. Unless you catch them right when they are exploring new resources, they will probably rebuff your attempts to connect with them. In this situation, try positioning yourself as complementing, not replacing, their current resource. For example, if they say, "We're all set," or "We're happy with our current partners," you can use the ART framework:

- **Acknowledge:** "That's great to hear that you have strong partners."
- **Relate:** "Most of our clients work with multiple resources to support their different needs."
- **Transition:** "Would you be open to exploring how we might complement what your current partners are offering?"

Though you can manage the objection perfectly during an outreach call, the prospect may not engage further. That's okay. You still benefit from making contact—you're no longer a stranger. When you reach back out, you can refer to a conversation you've had in the past as a way to warm up the outreach. For example, you might send an email stating, "Hi, Maya, you and I spoke a few months ago when you were working on X. You suggested I reach back out to you in September to set up a time to connect. Would you be available for a call this week?"

The second common scenario when you might be met with objections is when you're nearing a close. The objections you encounter will be specific to your actual service and expertise, but you can still craft an ARTful response. For example, if at this point your prospect says, "I'm not sure if you have the right experience" or "I'm not sure if you can do the job," try the following:

- **Acknowledge:** "I hear your concern around our experience in this space.
- **Relate:** "For an important initiative like this, I would also want to make sure that the firm I hire knows how to do this well."
- **Transition:** "Would it be helpful if I share with you why we're confident we can help you with your initiative and the ways in which you can experience the value we offer?"

Although objections never go away, they'll become rarer as your rainmaking skills further develop.

Practical Tip

The next time someone disagrees with you, acknowledge their point upfront instead of defending or explaining. Language you might use includes "Thank you for sharing that," "I can see what you're saying," or "That's an interesting point." Just make sure to say it in a curious, neutral tone, not a patronizing, judgmental one.

Managing Negotiations

Successful negotiations end in an agreement when the key goals of all parties are met. You're looking to partner with your prospect to solve a joint problem, not compete with them to get the best deal for yourself. Making sure the prospect—or client, if all goes right—walks away feeling positive about the negotiation is especially important. When you do win the engagement, you'll be working closely with this individual or their team, and you don't want any tension going into a new partnership. To ensure the needs of both sides are explored as you look to find an agreement, follow the six-step negotiation process.

Six-Step Negotiation Process

As shown in Figure 11.2, the six-step negotiation process consists of strategizing, setting the climate, gathering information, stating and justifying positions, bargaining, and reaching agreement.

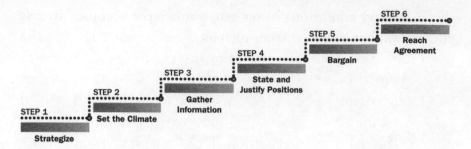

FIGURE 11.2 The Six-Step Negotiation Process

Step One: Strategize Be clear about your goals for the negotiation and your negotiating power. Consider the following:

- What is your starting offer?
- What push back are you expecting from the other side?
- What is your "walk-away" (the price and conditions at which it's not worth it for you to take on the project)?
- How much leverage do you have?
- What "currencies" do you have to trade?

Though we often think of currencies as financial, currencies in this context are anything of value that you'd be willing to give in exchange for a benefit for yourself. For example, access to additional resources; flexibility around duration and timing of engagement; the volume of work; fee terms, including upfront, overtime, and bonus incentives; and the potential for publicity, referrals, and introductions. You'll have your own set of currencies based on the services you and your firm offer.

It's important to distinguish between currencies and "existing conditions." Existing conditions are elements of what you offer that are valuable to the client but can't be negotiated away. These include your expertise, experience, industry knowledge, familiarity with the client, reputation in the marketplace, and consistent, high-quality work. It's important for you to discuss all of those throughout the sales process. Once you are in a negotiation, the client will have already factored these existing conditions into their offer. Now you can discuss currencies that can be traded, such as the experience level of the team staffed on the assignment, the amount of due diligence to be performed on the deal, the number of hours the client is willing to pay for, how much work on the matter will be handled by your team versus the client's internal team, and countless other elements. In a negotiation, focus on trading currencies, since existing conditions have already been factored.

When you're strategizing, it's critical to think about who's on the other side of the table. First, ensure you're negotiating with the decision-makers. Next, analyze their style and the style of their company. Is the negotiator direct and forceful, or laid back and friendly? Is the negotiator solidly established in the company, or are they looking to prove themselves? Are they pressured for time to complete this negotiation? The more you know about the other side and their motivations, the more you'll understand which currencies to trade to come to a win-win agreement.

Step Two: Set the Climate   Look to set a positive tone and remain conversational, affable, and optimistic. State the intention that you're confident you can find a way forward together. Create a collaborative environment by sitting next to each other, as opposed to across from each other, or choosing a setting that generally feels more relaxed, as compared to tense and uncomfortable. Try to avoid negotiating via email; it comes across as too transactional. Remember, client work in your field is all about relationships. Relationships require conversation.

Defuse confrontations as they arise. Research shows "that anger often harms the process by escalating conflict, biasing perceptions, and making impasses more likely. Angry negotiators are less accurate than neutral negotiators both in recalling their own interests and in judging other parties' interests."[1] By creating an understanding, congenial environment, your prospect will be more likely to collaborate than compete.

Step Three: Gather Information Continue to learn more about your prospect's end goal. What do they want? What's important to them? What's less valuable? What's currently happening at their company? As you gather this information, remain empathetic and open. Acknowledge everything the negotiator says but agree to as little as possible in the moment until you have time to reflect on how all of the elements discussed tie together. If the prospect presses you to agree on a specific issue, like an all-inclusive engagement price, you might say, "Let's get back to that one after we discuss the other issues on the table." If the other negotiator is evasive, providing broad, vague responses, be persistent in asking follow-up questions. You can't respond effectively and move the conversation forward without knowing what's really being offered by the other side.

Step Four: State and Justify Positions   Once you and the other negotiator determine the scope of the engagement at hand, you need to structure your proposal based on the parameters discussed and propose your fee. In many negotiations, you want the other person to make their offer first, so you know how far apart you are and can be more thoughtful in your counteroffer. But when selling your services, you'll likely need to put out the first price, which isn't always bad. The first offer can "anchor" the discussion.[2] If the fee for the services being discussed will be $150,000 over the course of six weeks, with seven team members at various rates, the client now has something to which they can respond. If your fee is reasonable and the scope of the engagement doesn't drastically change, you'll likely settle on a price in the vicinity of $150,000. How the number moves will depend on what currencies get traded on both sides.

Step Five: Bargain   Though all of these steps are part of the negotiation process, bargaining—the give-and-take stage—is what most people think of when they think of "negotiating." Throughout this step, inquire more deeply about the other party's stated position. Try to figure out which provisions are important to the other side and why. You might ask, "Can you help me understand the reason for. . .?" or "Would you be open to. . .?"

Bargaining is when the currencies you've identified in Step One come back into play. Make sure to prepare a list of currencies in advance so you have your bargaining chips ready. Think about what you can exchange that has solid value to the prospect but requires little effort or sacrifice on your part. These might be payment terms, the project timeline, caps on the number of hours to be spent on a deal, amount of time spent by associates versus partners, or access to additional experts who might need to be hired to get the work done.

In addition to currencies, the bargaining step is also when you need to think about concessions. Before you concede anything, make sure to get something in return (assuming you still want to do the deal). To that end, make your concessions conditional: If you say, "I'm willing to add in X," you have now committed to doing X regardless of whether you get anything in return. Instead, say, "If I could add in X, would you be willing to do Z?" Or, "If I could add in X, what would you be able to do?" Now X isn't on the table unless you get something in return.

Accept any concessions the negotiator gives you for free. If a concession is too difficult for you to give, don't be afraid to say, "I won't be able to do that." If the negotiator makes an unreasonable demand and then asks you for a concession, do not give them one. Throughout this process, maintain a reasonable point of view. Also, remember that most people offer concessions toward the end of a negotiation. Since that's the case, retain as many concessions for as long as possible so you can trade them at the very end.

Step Six: Reach Agreement   Reaching agreement is the final stage in the negotiation process, when both you and the prospect come together. Whenever you have multiple terms to negotiate, you're more likely to have fewer impasses if you negotiate them in one package than if you negotiate each point individually.[3] When you negotiate each item individually, if you get stuck on one, the negotiation ends. If you're able to negotiate terms as a package, you might overcome an impasse with one item by conceding another. This approach typically allows more wiggle room for both parties to come to an agreement in which they are better off.

In a successful negotiation, both of you are relatively satisfied and each party's position has improved. By creating a win-win situation, you and your new clients are more likely to negotiate together again in the future. When you are negotiating, remember to remain stoic, especially if you land a great deal. Don't celebrate or look too pleased with yourself. If you seem overly satisfied, or if you agree too quickly to an offer, the other side immediately feels like they left money on the table. That's not what you want—you want the other side to feel that they got a good deal, too. You should look pleased that you'll be able to work for the client, not excited that you closed the deal on terms good for you.

The Art of Pricing
During the negotiation process, one of the main areas where you will often get pushback is on pricing. Obviously, pricing is important—you need to price your services in a way that will

allow you to close the deal, but also provide long-term profitability. As discussed in Chapter 7, when possible, figure out your prospects' budget upfront so you can design a solution that fits within this important constraint. Unless you have already established deep trust with your prospects, you'll likely get a vague response from them when you ask about their budget. They may fear that they'll be taken advantage of if you know how much they are willing to spend. One way to reduce this fear is to ask them to share what they've paid for similar services in the past.

Conversely, they may ask you for your pricing before they learn more about your solutions or how you can add value. As mentioned in Chapter 7, this isn't necessarily a bad situation to be in, but you'll want to be careful not to price yourself out of the running, especially if the problem you're looking to solve is not yet clear. One way to still answer your prospect's request while preserving flexibility is to offer a range dependent on a variety of factors. This may be sufficient to get the conversation going.

When you can, tie your fee to the value you contribute. Your ability to do this depends on how directly your expertise can lead to measurable results. If your services lend themselves to calculating clear ROI for your client, then your fees should be a percentage of the measurable value you help your client generate. When you place your fees next to the potential return, it will make them look more reasonable than if you had offered them up alone. If the impact of your services is harder to measure because your work focuses more on the intangibles, you may be pegged to what your client is used to paying for such services, or a pricing structure tied to selling your time, like billable hours.

Think of ways to price your work so it will appeal to both you and the prospective client. For example, try offering tiered pricing, with good, better, and best options. Such pricing gives you flexibility and allows you to cater to different types of clients.

Research shows that when you offer multiple options, your clients focus more on selecting one of the choices in front of them instead of a binary yes-no decision.[4] The contrast between choices will also increase the attractiveness of one of your options, typically the "better" one.

You can also try selling an all-inclusive package upfront instead of charging à la carte for your services. When you charge for your services separately, although the dollar amount might seem smaller, the cost for your client to constantly evaluate whether or not they should pay for a certain service can create more dissatisfaction than if they paid for everything upfront.[5] If they pay for your services upfront, they can just focus on partnering with you for your service. (Of course, you'll need to watch out for scope creep and have clear guidelines when the work you're putting in exceeds the package that was paid for.) Despite these best practices, your specific prospect may dictate how they want you to structure your pricing. Some will require a rate card with each component broken out, and others may prefer you give them package pricing. Flex to your prospects' requirements, but when given an option, consider using the good, better, and best package approach.

A common question you may get asked after you share your pricing is, "Is that the best you can do?" What then typically follows is . . . silence. The hope here is that you'll negotiate with yourself in real-time. Be prepared for this question by knowing your own pricing structures and approach inside and out. Stand firm so you don't negotiate against yourself, but still remain flexible enough to work out a deal. One way to respond is to say, "Yes, this is our pricing based on what we discussed and the outcomes you want to achieve. Does this fit within your budget? If not, we can discuss adjusting the solution so it's in line with your budget."

Usually, if they were just using this question as a tactic to get a better price, the prospect will agree to your original pricing.

When they truly have an issue with your fees, they might share either other pricing they've seen or their actual budget. If they bring up lower pricing from a competitor, discuss whether the solutions and delivery resources are comparable. Offer to review the competitor's proposal to point out any differences. You might highlight additional services you're providing, your long-standing relationship with the company, or your experience in the industry. You'll also want to connect how those differences impact the outcome your prospect wants. As you have this conversation, you may find there are some adjustments you can make to your actual solution to bring down the price.

A similar question they may ask to get you to come down on your rates is "Why are your fees so high?" You can address this question with the trusty ART framework:

- **Acknowledge:** "It sounds like you have some concerns around how we priced this engagement."
- **Relate:** "If I were you, I would want to make sure I'm getting the right value for the fees. Can you share more details around your concern? What other pricing are you seeing?"
- **Transition:** "Would it be helpful if I share how we calculated our pricing?"

Whenever your prospect pushes back on price, they are really saying they don't see the additional value of your services when compared to lower-priced options. Price serves as a proxy for value. Your clients will evaluate price relative to what they find externally and what they benchmark internally. If your pricing is higher than average, you'll need to clearly show you are different and that it's still a better deal for them to engage you than to hire someone else, or to do it themselves. Most people do not call something expensive if they believe it is worth it.

Practice the Tactics

- Reflect on your current pursuits. Are you waiting for the client to get back to you? If so, what could you have done to keep the ball in your court around next steps?

- Reflect on two to three common objections you often hear, and use the Acknowledge, Relate, and Transition (ART) framework to manage them. To practice your delivery, video-record yourself sharing your response to ensure it sounds natural and sincere.

- List out the currencies you can use to negotiate with your clients. Identify the currencies your clients typically value that are of lesser value for you to trade.

- Find a real opportunity to negotiate this week and use the six-step negotiation process. This might be with a client, your own firm, or your wireless carrier. Note which steps you find most difficult.

- Study your pricing and see if you can offer a good, better, and best package to your clients, if you don't already structure your pricing that way.

- Imagine your client just challenged you on your pricing and said, "Why are your fees so high?" Practice aloud your response.

Protect Your Rainmaking Time

Chapter 12: Protect Your Rainmaking Time

If you execute your business development strategy well, you'll soon find yourself in an inevitable predicament: not having enough time. At first, being busy with client delivery almost sounds like a good problem to have. But as stressed earlier, rainmakers need to keep their pipelines full, continuously building their book of business. The more successful you are in generating business, the less time you will have to sell. Each successful client meeting leads to more non-selling follow-up work, including client service, engagement delivery, and general administration. In addition, you will have issues to resolve, people to manage, IP to create, associations to join, commitments to keep—it all adds up, and you'll find yourself being diverted from crucial business development activities.

Sometimes, you're pulled away from business development because you want to make sure everything goes just right when delivering the work you've put so much time and effort into selling in the first place. Other times, you have a blowout year and get swamped with client management activities or are flooded with billable work you have to manage because you're short staffed. Naturally, once you land your own clients, they will command your attention, and you will want to keep them happy. Unfortunately, if you don't actively protect your business development time, you'll find yourself overwhelmed with work that doesn't lead to more revenue.

Still, protecting your time to sell doesn't mean leaving your hard-won clients in the lurch. You're, of course, responsible for the execution, but to hit higher revenue numbers, you don't want to be mired in the technical work. You may still need to give guidance on highly specialized topics, but you should focus on continuing to build your book of business. Bringing in revenue is more valuable to you and your firm than the technical and administrative work your firm can hire someone else to do. And when you protect your rainmaking time, you stand a better chance at reaching your increasing revenue targets. But first, you need to have a clear appreciation for what work actually contributes to generating revenue.

Discerning Uptime from Downtime

Uptime is any time *spent with an Ideal Connection* to build a relationship and to create or advance revenue-generating opportunities. Downtime is any time that is not uptime, including time spent on activities that are related to the business development process. As a rule of thumb, downtime activities on their own won't lead to a sale, no matter how much of them you do. Wordsmithing a proposal, rehearsing a pitch, enhancing your online presence, or updating your Ideal Connections list are all downtime activities. Many of these tasks are important and, in a number of instances, absolutely critical, but they do not serve the same purpose as uptime activities. When you confuse the two, it is easy to feel as if you're spending a lot more time on business development than you actually are. Table 12.1 provides a clear summary of uptime and downtime activities.

As Table 12.1 shows, there are *many* more downtime activities than uptime ones. Although rainmakers seem to do thousands of different things at once, their success comes from doing the handful of revenue-generating activities thousands of times. By staying in uptime, you're availing yourself of potential opportunities, which should increase your chances of generating revenue. As a rainmaker, you should constantly focus on maximizing your uptime and managing your downtime.

Table 12.1   Uptime vs. Downtime Activities

Uptime Activities	Downtime Activities
• Direct client outreach and relationship building. Includes any conversation with a business professional that can potentially lead to a direct business opportunity or any conversation that is the result of referrals or introductions. • Engagement debrief to ask clients for feedback and referrals to their contacts and colleagues. • Live marketing activities with Ideal Connections in the room, including speaking engagements and showcases.	• Engagement delivery and client management and service. • Updating your CRM. • Researching industry topics or trends. • Creating content for websites, blogs, and social media. • Writing articles or whitepapers. • Prepping for meetings or speaking engagements. • Checking social media feeds. • Internal meetings and initiatives. • Strategizing, sharing best practices, or commiserating internally. • Crafting proposals or working on RFPs. (Though necessary, completing RFPs can often seem like a lot of data entry.) • Administrative work, such as submitting expenses, reviewing agreements, or filling out other forms. • Training and development (critical, but still downtime). • People management (essential for team building and scaling, but still downtime since you're not with a client). • Literally any other work not listed under uptime activities.

Maximize Uptime

To maximize your uptime, you need to focus on the highest value activities in which only you can engage. In selling your services, that uptime will mostly be based around live interactions with your Ideal Connections, especially prospects and clients. Though billable work may seem more important at times, beyond potentially improving your technical expertise, you don't gain as much value from just delivering your work. Billable hours are more visible and immediate than building relationships—and it's what your clients pay for—but you still need to carve out time to sell. If you don't take time away from your billable work, then that time has to come from somewhere else. Only you can decide how to best use your time, but there are specific tactics you can employ to start maximizing your uptime activities today.

At a minimum, aim to commit to at least a few hours of uptime each week. To pinpoint where you currently spend most of your time, take a look at your calendar for the past month. Now, estimate your hours spent in uptime versus downtime, using the guidelines in Table 12.1. If you're like most people, you'll be surprised to find that most of those hours are going toward downtime. This fact shouldn't come as a surprise. Many of us confuse downtime activities with uptime ones. A few of us may also de-prioritize uptime activities, especially if the time we're spending with Ideal Connections doesn't feel productive. Some of us may become distracted by non-selling work or simply forget about uptime because it's not urgent. To make it easier for you to stay in uptime, ingrain these important business development activities into your everyday routines and habits.

Create Cue-Based Plans

In *How to Change: The Science of Getting from Where You Are to Where You Want to Be*, Wharton Professor Katy Milkman suggests, "When you have a goal that you're afraid you might flake out on, you can create cue-based plans...just remember to consider the how, when, and where: How will you do it? When will you do it? Where will you do it? Be strategic about the cues you select—if you can, choose cues that are out of the ordinary."[1]

Cues remind us to take action, performing important activities we don't always follow through on. Instead of motivating ourselves or marshalling our willpower, we can design cue-based plans, so we don't have to decide whether or not to do something—when we see the cue, we automatically follow the rule we've set in place. To build these rules, you must articulate the uptime activity you will do, along with the time and place to do it, then create a noticeable cue that reminds you at that right place and time. For instance, every time you have a meeting rescheduled or end early (cue), you tackle an uptime activity, like calling a client whom you haven't spoken with in a while or following up with someone you met at a networking event (desired activity).

You may already have existing, reliable routines that you can lean on as cues for uptime activities. By tying your new habit to an existing one, you use your daily routines as cues. For example, to make a habit of daily client outreach, you might tie it to your current daily habit of drinking your mid-morning coffee. Stanford Professor B. J. Fogg recommends that this new habit come after the existing one. He also suggests specifying the last action of that routine. For example, instead of "After my morning coffee. . .," you would say, "After I sit down at my desk with my morning-coffee. . . ." Fogg suggests the following template: "After I (last action of existing routine), I will (new habit)."[2] So in the outreach example, your cue-based plan may be "After I sit down at my desk with my mid-morning coffee, I will call one client."

To start developing these cues, list your daily routines and connect your uptime activities to them. For example:

- After I finish checking my inbox in the morning, I will call two clients.
- After I return to my desk from lunch, I will follow-up with at least one person I recently met.

Start small. Come up with an easy-to-follow, cue-based plan and then track your progress. If you can consistently keep the rule without much effort, increase the frequency of the uptime activity or add more cue-based plans. Keep an eye on your total uptime from week to week to see if the plans are increasing your uptime activities. If they are not, reassess and experiment with some different cues until you find those that work best for you.

Gamify Uptime

When we try to convince ourselves to increase our uptime, we may emphasize how important uptime is to our career. Professor Milkman advises you might be better off looking for ways to make uptime activities fun, as opposed to just stressing their importance. Perhaps you reward yourself with a favorite afternoon snack after you complete a certain number of outreach activities. Make the reward something that reinforces your desire to do more outreach. The reward shouldn't be, "Once I connect with someone through a cold call, I can finally stop my selling for the day." You want a "Yes!" not a "Thank God that's over!" By creating clear rules and a way to win or lose, you can gamify uptime to keep yourself engaged.

I have one client who uses a points system. She assigns a point value for different types of sales activities and sets a goal to score four points every day:

- 1 point: Generate lead, referral, intro to a potential decision maker
- 2 points: Schedule a call or meeting with the decision maker
- 3 points: Meet with a decision maker to discuss an opportunity
- 4 points: Close a deal or get a clients' commitment to do business together

The points system accounts for the impact of the sales activity. If you try this approach, you'll notice that early on as you're building your book of business, you might have many one-point activities. As you get more seasoned and your contacts expand, you'll score more points through higher point activities (which also indicates you've become more productive with less time).

To up the ante, you might consider going for streaks. How many days in a row can you score a point or more? Since you'll be juggling many different activities, to help you keep this habit, give yourself flexibility, either by allowing yourself two emergency passes a week (when you have to skip the activity) or to make the points up the following day. The unexpected derailer is inevitable, and you want a way to allow yourself to keep your streak, despite any disruptions. Still, don't give yourself too much leeway—stay focused on uptime activities as much as possible despite client challenges or other unexpected emergencies.

Make Uptime Easy

Look for ways to make uptime activities easier. Start by removing any distractions. You might block out uptime on your shared calendar so no one schedules a meeting with you during that time. If you find your email inbox distracting because it pulls you into client service work, you may want to turn off notifications or only open your email after you've completed a few uptime activities that day. If you're tempted by a downtime activity while you're in uptime, don't deny it. Instead, try to "surf the urge," by giving yourself a 10-minute waiting period before doing that downtime activity.[3] You'll find that as you're waiting, you'll naturally remind yourself of the benefits of staying in uptime. The urge will dissipate and you'll get back to uptime.

You can also find ways to layer uptime activities on top of other activities you must do. For instance, if you have a long commute, you may use your travel time to catch up with one of your Ideal Connections. If you work with your team onsite at your client's office, instead of always meeting with your team for lunch, you may opt to meet with your client or other Ideal Connections in the area. These incremental and consistent changes can add up to help you maximize your uptime. Think outside of the box here, too. Perhaps you can build your network through community service opportunities. Or engage in social activities, like taking a cooking class or running a 10K race with one of your buyers, particularly if your relationship has developed into a friendship (as discussed in Chapter 8).

Practical Tip

If you're serious about staying in uptime, try using a commitment device, where you willingly and publicly take a penalty for not keeping your commitment.[4] The penalty has to be a consequence that you want to avoid. For example, you might tell your friends and co-workers that you're committing to canceling your HBO Max account for a year if you fail to complete a certain number of outreach activities (and you have to actually follow through).

Manage Downtime

In addition to maximizing uptime, another way to protect your rainmaking time is to manage downtime activities. As you become pressed for time, you'll find that activities that naturally don't have a lot of value begin to fall away. By making uptime an inviolable priority, it will help you crowd out other activities that matter less. One way to help you decide which downtime

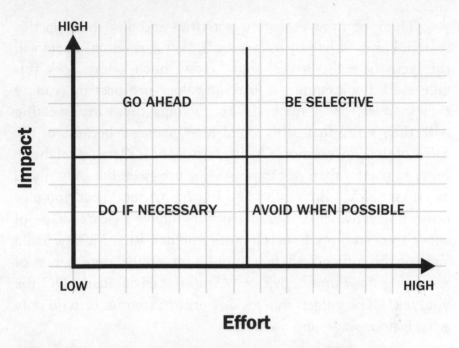

FIGURE 12.1 Impact vs. Effort Matrix

activities to stop is to list out all your downtime activities and plot them on an Impact vs. Effort Matrix (Figure 12.1).

Impact for a rainmaker comes from any activity that helps bring in business. Effort is the time, energy, and resources one needs to expend to complete the activity. Effort is unique to the individual. The same activity may be low effort for one person and extremely high effort for another (writing is a good example). For the high impact, low effort activities (upper left), you'll want to go ahead and tackle these downtime activities first. For high impact, high effort activities (upper right), be selective about what you take on because you won't be able to take on many. For low impact, low effort (bottom left) activities, only complete these if your clients or firm requires it. Similarly, but even more strictly, avoid low impact, high effort activities (bottom right) whenever possible.

Think of a few downtime activities and plot them on this matrix. For each activity, ask yourself, "What revenue impact will this activity really have?" and "How much effort does this take me?" For example, researching your prospect by reading their annual report might be more impactful when meeting with their CEO than with a mid-level manager because of the focus of the conversation. Creating thought leadership might be more impactful than researching your prospect, but only if you can do it quickly. Both effort and impact matter. When you plot downtime activities on the matrix, you'll have a clearer sense of those you can drop. Exec|Comm's founder, Rich McKay, had a sign on his office wall to remind him of the importance of managing downtime activities: "Avoid the trivial many, DO the vital few!" The golden rule for downtime activities is to do only what is necessary—and no more.

Increase Efficiency

Think about your downtime activities. Right off the bat, ask yourself, "What can I do to shorten the time I spend on them?" There are plenty of options. For example, when it comes to updating your CRM, or any other client databases, try entering just enough information to make the entry useful. It's easy to end up being comprehensive for the sake of being comprehensive. In most cases, however, you just need key info—important contacts, notable details, major issues to follow-up on, and next steps are enough. Similarly, researching, writing emails, prepping for meetings and pitches, and updating your online profile all may feel like uptime activities, but they aren't.

Obviously, some downtime is necessary to make the most effective use of uptime. The idea is to spend as little time as possible on downtime activities *while still achieving the results you want*. It is important to be prepared and to put your best foot forward, whether you're giving a talk, posting a video on social media, or publishing a thought leadership piece. But prep time is not the same as uptime. If you spend three hours creating and rehearsing your twenty-minute client presentation, that's only twenty minutes of uptime and three hours of downtime.

There are a number of approaches that can help you increase your efficiency with downtime activities. First, try to discern between which activities are productive and which might be a "nice to have," or are unnecessary all together. It helps to recognize when "good enough" is truly good enough. Spending an extra hour fiddling with a client pitch deck that may or may not be used during a meeting is likely not the best use of your time. Second, consider workshops that will help you became more skilled at completing your downtime activities. Yes, training is a downtime activity, but a critical one if it helps you better manage downtime and improve the quality of your uptime activities. A presentation skills workshop, for example, might help you reduce the time needed to create and prep for client pitches.

Third, you might lean on existing pitch deck templates, outreach emails, proposals, or engagement processes, repurposing work your organization has already done. If your firm doesn't have a way to centralize this knowledge, you'll want to create your own repository of commonly used resources. You can also leverage technology to help automate many of the administrative tasks you have to manage, along with research you may need to do. For example, you might leverage a CRM system like Salesforce to automatically generate a client call list, highlight client trigger events, or show you a dashboard tracking many of the metrics you learned in Part II.

You can also plan out when to best focus on uptime versus downtime activities. In Daniel Pink's book, *When: The Scientific Secrets of Perfect Timing*, he writes about optimal times for productivity based on humans' natural cycle—most people's moods rise in the morning, decline in early to mid-afternoon, and then shoot back up again in the early evening.[5] Make sure you schedule your uptime during those "high moods" times and avoid low energy times like the mid-afternoon. Not everyone will follow this same schedule—you may get your best work done in the mid-afternoon, or maybe you're a night owl and feel most productive when everyone else is asleep. Take note of your most productive, high-energy times throughout the day and save those for uptime.

Learn to (Nicely) Say "No"

Anytime you say "yes" to someone else, you are likely saying "no" to yourself. Learning to say "no" and setting boundaries are healthy ways to avoid downtime activities that don't serve you well. Say you're looking to build your business, but a colleague asks you to join the new office search committee. Though you'd love to help, you recognize this additional commitment—a downtime activity—will be quite time consuming. Still, it can be hard to say "no," especially when a colleague is asking for a favor. You may feel guilty for disappointing them, but don't see saying "no" as a rejection of the other person. Instead, recognize it as an affirmation of your own goals.[6] You are not *against* what is being asked; you are *for* what you are trying to achieve, in this case, sticking to your uptime activities and hitting your revenue targets.

When you decline, you can still show a willingness to help. For example, you can say, "You're welcome to X" or "I'm willing to Y" based on the request, or "I can't do it, but Z might be interested." For example, if your colleague invites you to a bi-weekly internal update meeting that is not critical for you, you might say, "Thank you for the invitation. I won't be able to commit to that. Would it be helpful if someone from my team represents us at the meeting?"

You can also use a soft "no," such as "let me check my calendar and get back to you" or "let me think about it, and I'll follow up next week." This will help you gauge if the other person is serious or if they will be able to find someone else to help with their request; if they seriously need you, they will come back to you. The point here is to be slow to say "yes," and quick to say "no."

Of course, exercise judgment when using these tactics to politely decline. In some cases, saying "no" might be detrimental to you even if it pulls you away from uptime. For example, when your boss or a key client asks you to perform a downtime activity, you need to understand the consequences of refusing and make sure you can manage those consequences properly. If you say "no" to your bosses too often, they might feel you're at capacity and pass an incoming lead to someone else; if you say "no" to clients too often, they may decide to work with someone who has more capacity. When you set boundaries well, you'll find that fewer people come to you with ad hoc requests.

Build Leverage through Others

No matter how efficient you become, you'll still hit a capacity issue if you continue to grow your book of business. To help, you'll want to purposefully build a team to better scale your abilities. Start by listing your key activities. Then highlight the ones that only you can do because of your expertise and relationships. Next, note the activities that can be done by others equally well, if not better. Broadly, you might outsource much of your client management and engagement delivery activities to competent team members. You can also leverage your administration, marketing, and business development functions to help with other downtime activities like researching prospects, warming up cold leads, crafting pitch emails, building presentation decks, or updating your CRM.

If you have already built a strong reputation and relationship delivering work for your clients, you may find it difficult at first to add new team members into the mix. Many people fear giving responsibility away to junior staff or other colleagues because they worry the relationships they've built may be negatively affected. KPMG Deal Advisory and Office Managing Partner Don Zambarano says, "One of the hardest things to do in the professional services career is getting from others what you expect getting from yourself." You might think it's hard to find someone who will treat your clients right. If you're bringing someone else in, maybe you worry they may not be as responsive as you are to your clients' needs, or they may not put in the same amount of care and effort as you do in building relationships. You might think no one can do this type of work as well as you can. "And it comes from a place of empathy and compassion for the client," Zambarano points out. "It's not because you don't trust the person doing the work, it's because you care so much for the client."

But Zambarano believes concerns over jeopardizing client relationships are unfounded. "I've learned that's just not true," he says. "That was something that restricted me because I didn't want to mess up any of my client relationships." He also reminds us that "first off, it's not your client relationship, it's your firm's client relationship. Second of all, how do you know they're not going to help you to develop a better relationship with your client?" Zambarano has had this exact experience, in which he's introduced his team members to clients, and they've hit it off. "I've found that when I relinquish control a bit and tap into the talent of our people, they often bring a different perspective and skillset, which improves the overall value delivered and relationship with the client. They're quicker, they use the tools better, they bring a different point of view." He tells would-be rainmakers to be careful, of course, and stay involved, but that they probably don't need to be *as* involved as they are right now.

When you start leveraging your team, be selective about your participation. Pinpoint the activities that may still be more effective for you to do. Beyond uptime activities, you might offer to take part in some of the delivery work where your deep expertise is needed. Zambarano suggests taking the lead to check in with your clients about your team's performance and to take ownership over any major issues. "I believe in having an open dialogue with my clients, asking them how is 'so and so' working out and what they think about them. They'll be honest with you." For example, if the personality fit is off, maybe you make a switch and have another supporting team member handle the delivery. The main idea is to know the highest value activities only you can complete because of your expertise, relationships, and unique value. Find others who can help you with the rest. Preserve your time for prospecting, and lean on your team to continue building your business.

Practice the Tactics

- Review the last two to four weeks of your work calendar. Note how much time you're spending in uptime. For this coming week, create one cue-based plan to help you increase your uptime activities during work hours.
  - Ask yourself, "How will I do it? When will I do it? Where will I do it?"
  - Leverage Professor Fogg's template: "*After I* (last action of existing routine), *I will* (new habit)."
- Try the points system for the next two weeks. The goal is to score four points every day:
  - 1 point: Generate lead, referral, introduction to potential decision maker

- 2 points: Schedule a call or meeting with the decision maker
- 3 points: Meet with a decision maker to discuss an opportunity
- 4 points: Close a deal or get a client's commitment to do business together

- Figure out your high-energy and low-energy times and schedule one uptime activity on your calendar during one of the high-energy times.

- Plot your downtime activities for the upcoming week or month using the Impact vs. Effort Matrix in Figure 12.1. Look at your necessary downtime activities and try cutting down the time they take by 10 percent. You can stop doing some of them, more effectively do them, or outsource them.

  - Think of a few downtime activity requests you often receive. Practice saying "no" to each of these activities. You may want to record yourself saying "no" to review your tone and approach.

  - Offload one downtime activity to someone on your team this week or just stop doing it altogether.

CHAPTER

13

Stay Relevant

Chapter 13: Stay Relevant

At Exec | Comm, our business is highly personal. As we help our clients enhance the way they communicate and connect with others, we often hear about their fears and insecurities. They trust us with their vulnerabilities as we help them step out of their comfort zone. For forty years, we've served our clients by being in the same room with them, coaching them, and coaxing them along their growth path. In 2020, the COVID-19 pandemic forced us to rethink how we could support them since face-to-face interactions were no longer an option. To further complicate the situation, at the start of the pandemic, many of our clients had to focus on the survival of their business, not on developing their people. They postponed leadership development programs, deferred promotions, and canceled coaching for their conference speakers. Training, in general, became a lower priority.

We had to quickly assess the situation and figure out what our clients needed during this transition and how to support them. We recognized that for some of our more traditional clients, working from home was new. Their leaders wanted guidance on how to manage remote teams and run effective virtual meetings. Their team members weren't sure how best to communicate and collaborate in this new environment. Different functions also had their own unique issues. For example, given the circumstances, salespeople weren't sure if it was appropriate to reach out to clients during that time. They were also concerned about how best to build relationships in a purely virtual environment.

To respond to our clients' changing priorities, we revised our content to include advice on working remotely, used new technologies to deliver engaging content, and designed novel approaches to effectively build skills. With this updated menu of virtual programs, our clients re-engaged us to help their people work effectively during an unprecedented time. We won business from both existing and new clients because several of our competitors were unwilling or unable to adapt as quickly or effectively. By changing our approach and continuing to learn, we remained relevant, providing solutions to unique problems that had been unforeseen just a few months earlier.

As discussed, unlike professionals who sell products, in professional services, *you* are the product your clients buy. You have a responsibility to keep improving your skills to meet their changing needs. As a rainmaker, the tactics you use will continue to evolve, even as the mindset and core strategies remain constant. Circumstances change, new technologies replace old ones, clients' buying methods shift. You may, for example, need to build a relationship with someone without ever meeting them in-person. Or, you might have to leverage new software platforms to automate your client outreach based on real-time trigger events. To help you thrive no matter how the world changes around you, you need to keep learning, sharpening the saw and getting better at what you do and how you do it. Continuous, intentional learning gives you an ability to effectively incorporate new skills and tactics, allowing you to stay relevant as you build your book of business. Knowing what to learn, when, and how to go about it—along with the ability to apply your know-how effectively—will provide an edge over your competition and create more opportunities with potential and existing clients.

Learn with Intention

The late Professor K. Anders Ericsson, a leading researcher on expertise and human performance, believed that the "right sort of practice carried out over a sufficient period of time leads to improvement."[1] He coined this approach *deliberate practice*. In deliberate practice, we pinpoint the activity needed to improve our performance, repeatedly perform this activity, and receive feedback on our progress. Instead of practicing what we're good at, we practice what we're bad at. It's the struggle that helps us grow. Whether you build valuation models, audit financial statements, or play on the PGA tour, you likely recognize the role of deliberate practice.

Finding what skills to develop requires you to be attuned to the fringes of your competence. Approaching a new frontier of your competence is both scary and exhilarating. If you're a skier, it's like the first time down a black diamond slope. You're fully engaged in the moment, and even then, you're not sure if you can make it through without falling. You are striving for laser-like focus when you practice. Ideally, you would have an instructor show you how to best navigate the terrain. Activities that you can do easily without effort, like the green trails in skiing, won't help you grow.

To become a rainmaker, you need to be purposeful about the skills you develop. You want to focus on those that will help you stay relevant to your clients and to the market. Once you determine the specific skills to develop, though, you can intentionally turn knowledge into expertise by following the Cycle of Intentional Learning, a three-step cycle of gaining knowledge, applying that knowledge, and reflecting on the results (as shown in Figure 13.1).

The cycle can be broken down as such:

- **Step 1: Gain.** From a skill-building perspective, start by considering your options for learning that skill. You might attend a training program, read a book, or shadow high performers to pick up best practices. This first step accelerates your learning—by following a proven path, instead of making it up as you go, you bypass common mistakes.

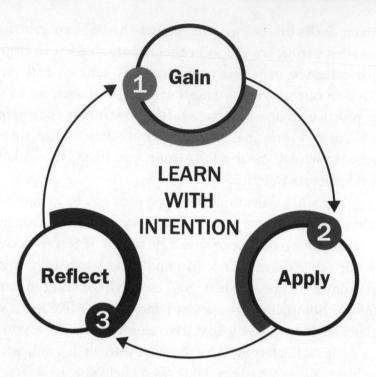

FIGURE 13.1 The Cycle of Intentional Learning

- **Step 2: Apply.** Once you've internalized the know-how, you'll want to apply the key concepts in real-life situations, helping you build the skill. By applying what you're learning, you also embed this new knowledge. For example, when you get stumped by a question in a real meeting, you will likely go find the answer as soon as the meeting ends. You will then remember that answer more deeply in the future than if you were caught off guard with a question in a hypothetical role play.

- **Step 3: Reflect.** Based on the results of your efforts and feedback from senior colleagues, your manager, or others in a position to help you, reflect on what you've learned. You might recognize a skill gap that requires further practice or decide to adjust your approach as a better fit for you and the situation. These new insights refine your knowledge in step one, which you will apply in your next interaction, helping to perpetuate the cycle.

To be successful over the long-term, repeat this three-step cycle for any skill you want to learn. Before your next interaction with a client, for example, ask yourself, "How can I apply the skill I want to improve?" If you're working on your listening skills, you may want to consider how you'll demonstrate more active listening in your upcoming client meeting. Like building a muscle, you must put in the repetitions, using the right form, and increase the difficulty with each set. The more reps you can complete within a given amount of time, and the more feedback you receive on how to improve your form, the faster you'll be able to master those skills and move on to others.

Step 1: Gain Knowledge

Continuous learning is important; continuous learning in the right direction is critical. What you're really looking for in this stage of the cycle is an understanding of what knowledge you need to acquire to stay relevant to your clients. Though learning "just for the sake of learning" is personally satisfying and enriching, when it comes to helping your prospects and clients, you want to be deliberate in learning new skills or approaches that will be valuable to them. To guide your development, there are two visual roadmaps that can help you decide the knowledge and skills to build upon and when: S-curves and T-shapes.

S-Curves

S-curves have been used in various disciplines to show the natural course of skill development.[2] Growth in a particular skill starts slowly, then ramps up before hitting a plateau. To master any skill, you need to invest time upfront to learn the basics before adding value and seeing results. Once you have a firm grasp of the fundamentals and apply them across different situations, your competence begins to rise quickly. You move from understanding what must be done to actually doing it without as much effort. As you reach mastery, your growth starts to plateau since most situations you encounter will be familiar to you and in your comfort zone (see Figure 13.2). You are likely nearing the top of your skills S-curve when you can perform a skill well with little preparation or mental attention.

People hit plateaus at work all the time. Someone might have 15 years of experience, but if the skills they have been using

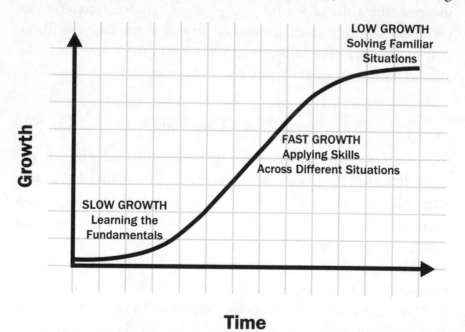

FIGURE 13.2 Ride the S-Curve of Mastery

are the same ones they learned after their first three years of work, then they're only spreading those three years of experience over 15 years. Your clients are discerning and may already work with other professionals who provide similar services to yours. They can tell the difference between someone's sophistication of thinking, which is gained by years of growth, and someone who is technically proficient but pedestrian in their approach. Like Irish Playwright Oscar Wilde quipped, "With age comes wisdom, but sometimes age comes alone."[3]

Once you reach an acceptable level of competence, you may go on autopilot and find yourself just going through the motions, no longer pushing yourself to improve. If that's the case, your clients are likely satisfied with your work but probably not delighted. To support your clients' evolving needs, you must continuously improve. If your skills plateau, you will also face more competition as others, including your clients, learn how to do what you do. To overcome this plateau and to continue growing your expertise, you need to disrupt yourself by boldly jumping to the next S-curve, as shown in Figure 13.3.[4] This "jump" can only take place when you innovate your approach with new insights or capabilities. If it doesn't require much effort for you to deliver your service to your clients now, you're ready to make the leap.

Research has shown that high-performing organizations jump S-curves to maintain their elite status.[5] When possible, follow their lead, and proactively choose when to jump to your next S-curve. If you wait too long, you'll find that your firm, your competitors, the market, or unforeseen disruptions (such as an international pandemic) will force you to the next S-curve, whether you're ready or not.

From an individual's standpoint, you might benefit from spending 10–20 percent of your knowledge acquisition and skill

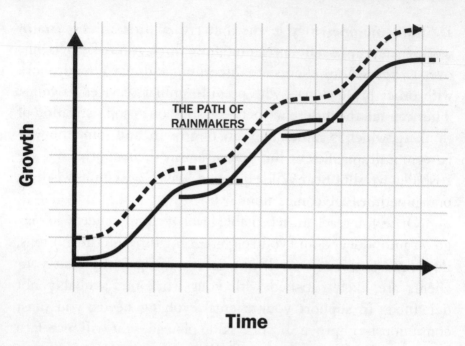

FIGURE 13.3 Disrupt Yourself by Jumping S-Curves

development efforts on exploring innovative or new approaches even when there isn't an immediate market need. For example, if you consult for traditional financial services firms, you might devote some time to developing your knowledge in the fintech space. If you're looking to innovate your client outreach activities, you may hire a digital marketer to better raise your Ideal Connections' awareness of who you are or use customer analytics to decide the right time to reach out. Such efforts will help you keep an eye on the innovative changes in your business that can help you better serve your client.

T-Shape

To complement your deep technical expertise, consider broadening your expertise across various topics, diversifying your knowledge and abilities. This broader perspective exposes you to additional frameworks to solve your clients' existing and future problems. It can also help you recognize opportunities you might otherwise miss. With more tools in your toolbox, you equip yourself with what you need to continue supporting your clients as their needs evolve.

Wharton Professor Adam Grant recommends diving deep in one specific area and broad in many as a path to being more creative.[6] This combination of mastering one trade, but being a jack of all others, is what forms the T-shape, shown in Figure 13.4.

The T-shape can also be applied to your industry knowledge. You've likely already developed strong institutional knowledge

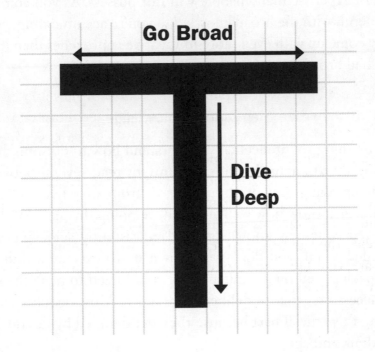

FIGURE 13.4 Be T-shaped

and contacts within specific industries; to further your development, broaden your exposure in others. As your industry expertise becomes more T-shaped, you can leverage the best practices from diverse industries to innovate your current offerings.

As the world continues to trend toward more uncertainty at an ever-faster pace, you may hear some people advocate for being a generalist instead of a specialist. They reason that committing to developing depth in one area may be risky—what if that expertise becomes obsolete? However, becoming an expert does not mean being stuck in your ways. True experts keep evolving their craft. Depth gives you the ability to improvise and remain agile because you can draw from more experiences relevant to your clients. It also helps you differentiate yourself as having a level of expertise many people will not possess. As you combine that depth with the broad knowledge you're accumulating, you'll likely come up with even more innovative approaches than if you only had broad expertise.

Step 2: Apply Knowledge

It's one thing to intellectually understand how to do something, and another to actually do it. You might read several books on public speaking, but until you get in front of a live audience, you'll never know how well you're developing this skill. Without applying your new knowledge and consistently achieving your intended result, you don't really own it. To execute a skill like rainmaking well on a regular basis, you'll need to push through the necessary grind of deliberate practice. Most people give up during this crucial part because they get derailed by discomfort, boredom, and ego.

When mastering any skill, you will begin outside your comfort zone, and you may stay there for quite some time. If you're not struggling, you're probably not growing. For some, this struggle might mean putting in an extra hour or two to prepare. For others, it may mean doing well one day but failing another day, always uncertain about their level of performance. No one likes to struggle. No one wants to feel like a failure. That's why it's so tough to build true expertise. But if building expertise was easy, experts would get paid a lot less.

Resist the natural pull to stay in your comfort zone. If you stop taking risks, you stop learning. The longer you remain in one place, the more time you give everyone else to catch up to you. And, as discussed in Chapter 12, as you succeed, your time will continue to become limited. Intentional learning takes time, so you have to prioritize the opportunities that will continue to sharpen your skills. Don't let a month go by without refining your craft. Review your work from a year or two ago. Are you slightly embarrassed with some element of it? If not, you may not be growing fast enough. If you're barely breaking a sweat at the gym, there is a good chance you are not making much progress. As you think about your last few client engagements, what remains difficult for you? If you feel it's easy to do your job right now, then you are probably nested in your comfort zone.

Sometimes, this struggle to apply what you're learning may come less from difficulty and more from boredom. Yes, learning new skills can be exciting, but deliberately practicing them over and over again until they're nearly second nature can become tedious. When studying experts across multiple disciplines, Roger Kneebone, the researcher on experts mentioned earlier in the book, notes, "The reality is that in any job there's a lot that's tedious, but it just has to be done. Nobody is entitled not to be bored. Unless you find ways of accepting that, you're likely to have a hard time. Yet, in our climate of immediate gratification and continual stimulation, coping with tasks that are inherently boring is becoming a lost art." He continues, "The boring bits are part of the work. Bypass them and you lose something essential."[7] There are no shortcuts to success, and sometimes there aren't scenic routes, either. When you feel bored and the process is tedious, stick with it because the payoff will be worth it.

And then there's ego. Being a seasoned professional, you're already considered an expert by your existing clients and your firm, and you're used to applying your expertise in an effortless way. Learning something new forces you to become a beginner again. Everything will seem difficult, and you won't know what you're doing. This lack of competence may feel dissonant with your self-image as an expert. You may become self-conscious and start doubting the value of becoming an amateur all over again. When you want to retreat back into your comfort zone, remember that the struggle in learning new skills doesn't hurt your expertise—it enhances your expertise. At any given time, if you feel like a beginner at something, you know you're growing. And as you apply what you learn, you provide more value for your clients.

To push beyond these derailers, put yourself in situations that force you to practice your developing skills in real-world settings. If you are working on your leadership skills, for example, find a role at work that allows you to lead others. If you don't want to take the risk at your job, find lower-stakes opportunities to practice. For example, you might offer your time at a non-profit where you can lead a team of volunteers to apply the leadership tactics you're learning. The more you apply the skill in real situations, the more you will learn about your abilities, strengths, and necessary improvements.

To help you survive the grind of deliberate practice, accept it as a critical part of the journey as you apply your newly forming knowledge. Be clear on what you want so you have the staying power to be the best at what you do. In time, apply your knowledge to more challenging opportunities, so you can further expand your skillset and keep growing. Unlock your potential through the skills you develop; develop your skills through the knowledge you apply.

Step 3: Reflect on the Results

Reflection is the *work* of learning. True learning occurs when you reflect on the results of your plan and how well you executed it. It's easy to neglect this last essential step. When we're pressed for time, it's easier to move on to the next task without thinking about how we did on the last one. We keep doing what we're doing. The time to pause and reflect on our actions seems like a luxury we can't afford. But, when we don't reflect on our work, our growth, and our capabilities, we risk wasting our energy and potential, doing the same things we've always done.

To reflect effectively, take any conversation, task, strategy, or action and compare what you expected to happen with what actually happened. If the reality consistently matches your expectation, then you know your approach is working. When you don't get the result you expected, you need to either adjust your expectations or adjust your approach going forward. For example, let's say you expected to reach out to ten clients this week but only contacted three. Reflecting on why you didn't hit your goal will inform you of a gap you may have to fill. Perhaps you need to learn how to organize your client information better or manage your other tasks more effectively to make time for client calls.

No matter the situation, think about what you could have done differently. If you feel like a client conversation didn't land as you'd hoped, ask yourself, "What was my key focus for this interaction, and how did I perform on achieving that outcome?" Or "What did I do well? What could I do better? What did I assume to be true that turned out to be false?" If possible, record yourself during an interaction so you can go back and review where you made mistakes and where you could improve.

Such self-reflective feedback will fuel your development, but feedback from outside sources is also important. Most people tend to avoid feedback since they often associate it with having done something incorrectly. When you hear your manager say, "Can I give you some feedback," you probably say, "Sure, that sounds great," but are likely thinking, "Uh-oh, what did I do wrong?" We typically want to hear what a good job we're doing, not what a *better* job we *could* be doing. But to reflect on what we're learning and how we're applying our new knowledge, we need to hear the truth about our performance from trusted sources. Without feedback, we stunt our growth and risk developing ineffective or irrelevant skills.

One of the best sources of feedback will be your clients. Though this seems obvious, many of us think to only ask for their feedback after an engagement. What you really want, however, is a good pulse on how your clients are feeling about your performance once they've hired you. Clients will rarely tell you you're "no good" in the moment—they just won't engage you for future opportunities if they're dissatisfied with your work. You want to make sure you uncover any dissatisfaction or confusion early on when you have the chance to resolve it. To do so, ask the following questions during or after any engagement:

- "What's your assessment of how things are going?"
- "What should my team and I *start* doing that will further enhance your experience?"
- "What should my team and I *continue* to do?"
- "What should my team and I *stop* doing?"

You might ask these questions more often at the start of a relationship, then move to more periodic check-ins. At the minimum, set up a midway-point check-in and a post-engagement check-in. You might also ask for feedback following a milestone deliverable. In addition to their responses, you can also pay attention to their actions and interactions with you as a form of feedback. For example, if they engage you for other deals, they likely appreciate the quality of your work. When they negotiate hard against you, they are likely questioning your value. Stay attuned to such signs.

The more immediate the feedback, the faster you'll learn. When you play an instrument, if you hit a wrong note, you know it in the moment. This feedback allows you to adjust while you practice. In business development, there is typically a delay between your selling activities and the actual revenue you generate. At the same time, you can still receive some form of immediate feedback no matter the situation. For example, when you meet with a client to walk through your proposal, you may gauge their interest in your solution through their body language and the quality of their questions.

In addition to clients, it's helpful to ask your colleagues for feedback. For instance, you can have them join you on a client meeting. To prime them beforehand, ask them to focus on the skill you've been working on. This extra step will allow the observer to pay closer attention to what you're practicing and offer you more specific and meaningful feedback afterward. As you receive feedback, ask for details related to observable behaviors. For example, if you received feedback that you came across as tentative, ask, "What specific behavior, if any, did you see that gave you that impression?"

To receive high-quality feedback, make it safe for the other person to be candid with you. If you react to feedback by defending your actions or blaming others or the circumstances, they will likely stop sharing constructive feedback—it's not worth their effort. Recognize that those who do not care about you or your success have little incentive to give you feedback. It's more work and often uncomfortable pointing out areas in which others need to develop. Signal your openness to their perspective with a simple "thank you," or by asking a question that shows you are truly interested in learning from their observation.

Thanking someone for their feedback doesn't mean you have to agree with it. You are just acknowledging their critique and appreciating their investment in you. If you are truly open, you will likely find something valuable in any feedback you receive. To build a reputation as someone open to feedback, take every opportunity to incorporate that feedback. By addressing constructive feedback, you fast-track your growth.

Practical Tip

Ask one of your rainmaking colleagues this week for feedback on your business development activity. Try to identify at least one activity you might consider starting or stopping to become more effective at generating revenue.

Quality feedback helps to perpetuate the Cycle of Intentional Learning. You take the *knowledge you gained* from the feedback, *apply* it to the next situation, and *reflect* on whether your result was better than it was before. You can't rest on your laurels, though—you need to keep learning, keep improving. In many ways, effective business development is about service to others. You have an expertise that can help your clients go where they want to go faster. If you aren't effective at selling that expertise, not only are they missing out, but you and those around you also miss out. When you have a thriving book of business, you create opportunities for yourself, your team, and your firm. By continuing to learn, focusing on your client, and doing great work, your clients will become your fans, champions, and advocates, allowing you to continue bringing in business.

Practice the Tactics

- Choose one professional skill that would be of value to your clients to start intentionally learning this week. Use the Cycle of Intentional Learning.

- Review your work calendar, and measure how much time you spent on developing yourself last month, last quarter, last year. What adjustments, if any, would you like to make to help you stay sharp?

- Reflect on your technical expertise and where you are on your current S-Curve. Is it time to jump to the next one?

- How is your T-shape developing? Do you need to go broader or deeper? Identify two skills in addition to your main area of expertise that you can build upon.

- What are the most recent client needs you're hearing? Decide how that will impact what skill you want to focus on developing next.

- Ask a colleague for feedback on a specific skill that you're working on right now. If possible, get feedback about that skill from a current client as well. See where that feedback overlaps and how you can apply what you've learned.

END OF PART III:
Tactics Matter

The tactics covered throughout Part III complement each other and, together, create the core of the rainmaker's skill set. To use these tactics as a cohesive set, and have them at the ready in any interaction, you first need to develop them through practice. Whenever you practice, you must isolate and drill specific skills before pulling them all together. It's like in tennis: You start with learning how to grip the racquet. Then you learn how to move your feet to position yourself well. Once you know how to move your feet, you practice your groundstrokes, net volleys, and serving, hitting hundreds of balls, until you feel comfortable. Next, you play a practice game to pull theses skills together. All of this practice comes together so you're ready for the actual competition. It's no different for rainmakers—the tactics throughout Part III play off of and enhance one another.

Your reputation sells for you, so you'll want to begin *building a trusted reputation* as soon as possible. Your personal brand can warm up outreach efforts and bring opportunities to you directly, but only if you first demonstrate the value you offer. To build your reputation, grow your network, and win business, you need tactics to *communicate care, competence, and collaboration* in all of your interactions. By understanding how to focus the conversation on the other person and make the best use of their time, they'll likely want to keep interacting with you. As you're developing your brand and ability to connect with others, you'll convert more prospects to clients when you become skilled at *driving the process forward*. As you become successful in building up your book of business, you'll lean on the tactics to *protect your rainmaking time* so you can further grow both your revenue and your team. And to continue your long-term success as a rainmaker, you have to *stay relevant*, and learn how to learn, to ensure you keep up with new innovations and strategies to meet your clients' evolving needs.

Developing these tactics requires consistency and patience. You won't get them all down in one day, and even once you're a seasoned rainmaker, you'll still need to sharpen them as new technologies and best practices come out. When learning anything, it takes time, and failure is a part of the process. As former US President Barack Obama says, "The point is, if you are living your life to the fullest, you will fail, you will stumble, you will screw up, you will fall down. But it will make you stronger, and you'll get it right the next time, or the time after that, or the time after that."[1] Rainmaking is a path to live your professional life to the fullest, and when it comes to tactics, if you keep at them, you will get there.

Conclusion

Throughout my career, I've seen a lot of talented, would-be rainmakers give up too easily. Much of their potential was unrealized because they were unwilling or unable to strongly advocate for their services, their firm, and most importantly, themselves. Maybe they were afraid of failure or had a distorted view of what rainmaking requires. Whatever the reason, they never gave business development a true shot. Many of them could have excelled, and in the process, helped not only themselves, but a lot of other people reach their aspirations. Whether in investment banking, management consulting, accounting, architecture, investment management, research, law, or any other professional service, there are always more reasons to tell yourself why you shouldn't try sales than why you should.

But, deep down, you *do* want to try—and not only try but succeed. And no matter how you might feel the deck is stacked against you, you *can* succeed. In doing so, you enhance your life, the lives of your clients, and in turn the lives of your clients' employees and customers. If you believe in the value of what you offer, and you manage to bring what you offer to the marketplace, *everyone* wins. As shown throughout the pages you've just read, effectively selling your expertise boils down to serving others. If you have a willingness to serve others, the openness to learn, and the fortitude to keep going, you can become a rainmaker.

As you set out, or continue, on your rainmaking journey, your success will depend on how much other people *want* to work with you. To make sure they do, you want to consistently and systematically build relationships with your Ideal Connections. When that happens, they will regularly think of you for their needs, and the needs of others, and trust you to help them solve their problems and achieve their goals. As they share their needs with you, remain focused on your Ideal Connections, and show that you care about them and are competent to help them succeed. Sometimes it will take a while until a concrete opportunity arrives, but as discussed, although you want to be impatient with your business development activity, you want to be patient with your results, all the while evolving your expertise to stay relevant to your clients.

To help you take stock of your own development, complete the Rainmaker's Checklist, shared at the end of this section. You might find it helpful to revisit this list once a quarter to help you track your progress. If you picked up this book because you weren't sure whether you could be successful generating revenue or you were half-hearted about the endeavor, I hope you walk away not only feeling encouraged, but expecting to win. I hope you've picked up a few good tips reading this book, but no matter what you learn, and where you learn it from, remember this advice from Bruce Lee in *Wisdom for the Way*: "Absorb what is useful, discard what is useless, and add what is specifically your own." As you blaze your own path forward, I would love to hear what you've learned and how you've refined these strategies and skills to serve your clients. If you think my firm and I can be helpful as you or your team continue to grow, don't hesitate to reach out.

Being a rainmaker, like being an expert, is a lifelong pursuit. The more you expand at the edges of what you're able to do, the more you'll contribute to your clients and the world. Making the